Popular Religion in Restoration England

University of Florida Monographs
Social Sciences No. 59

Popular Religion in Restoration England

C. John Sommerville

A University of Florida Book

The University Presses of Florida
Gainesville / 1977

Library of Congress Cataloging in Publication Data

Sommerville, Charles John, 1938–
    Popular religion in Restoration England.

    (University of Florida monographs : Social sciences ;
no. 59)
    "A University of Florida book."
    Includes bibliographical references and index.
    1. Christian literature, English—History and
criticism. 2. England—Church history—17th century.
3. England—Intellectual life—17th century. I. Title.
II. Series: Florida. University, Gainesville. University of Florida monographs : Social sciences ; no. 59.
BR756.S65   242   77–7618
ISBN 0–8130–0564–7

TYPOGRAPHY BY MODERN TYPOGRAPHERS, INCORPORATED
CLEARWATER, FLORIDA

PRINTED BY STORTER PRINTING COMPANY, INCORPORATED
GAINESVILLE, FLORIDA

Acknowledgments

Among the many who have given encouragement and help with this project, I should like especially to thank Professors Henry Horwitz, Paul Seaver, Ward Wilson, and the Rev. Dr. Geoffrey Nuttall. My wife, Susan, has helped materially at several points in the study, as well as sharing more generally in living with this topic. And I am indebted to Professors Aubrey Williams, Samuel S. Hill, Corbin Carnell, and Michael Braun for suggestions on the manuscript.

Additional thanks must go to the University of Florida Graduate School for making possible the publication of this monograph.

To my parents

W.B.S. and K.M.S.

Contents

1. The Study of Popular Religion

One of the historian's greatest challenges is to try to say with assurance what "the common man" thought or felt or hoped in some past period. It is a question that often occurs to the general public, and frequently the historian's answer must simply be an explanation of the difficulties involved. For indeed the task may be hopeless, when it means characterizing the mentality of the more inarticulate elements of society and dealing with assumptions that "went without saying." Still, these difficulties have not always deterred historians from generalizing, sometimes almost unconsciously, about the attitudes of various groups and ages. In religious history, specifically, those whose study has concentrated on the development of doctrine and institutions by the clerical estate have often ventured statements about the sentiments of whole societies. And these have usually been rather casual inferences, however inspired and convincing they may be. It is possible, however, to introduce a greater rigor into the study of popular religion.

"Popular religion," for purposes of the present study, is taken to be those religious beliefs and attitudes favored by the lay public, as shown in the favorite reading of a literate society with a cheap and prolific religious press. England had high levels of literacy and book production in the late seventeenth century, as we shall see. It was also a period for which we have adequate means of determining the relative popularity of different books, and even the extent of their popularity. But, more important, it was a time which is increasingly seen as crucial in England's religious and intellectual development.

"We live in a printing age, wherein there is no man either so vainly, or factiously, or filthily disposed, but there are crept out . . . all sorts [of] unauthorized authors, to fill and fit his humor," lamented one Englishman in 1591, "and if a man's devotion serve him not to goe to the Church of GOD, he neede but repayre to a Stationer's shop and reade a sermon of the divels."[1] In this despair is the historian's hope, for the rise of printing had given the laity a way to register its approval in matters of doctrine. A study of sermons even for the medieval period might show something of the popular mind, supposing that they were pitched at the level of a general audience. But after the advent of printing, a study of those sermons which required the most numerous reprintings can give us a much more precise record of what the book-buying public thought it would approve and enjoy. It was possible to go home from an uncongenial sermon and take down some author more to one's taste, choosing from among literally thousands of religious titles. "Private reading maketh the publike ministrie more profitable," wrote one Puritan, because it "inableth us better to judge of the Doctrines taught."[2] But it could also make the public ministry superfluous, for the very existence of these books was a challenge to the corporate instruction of the Church and the authority of the clergy. Books were creating a new order of family prayers and private devotions, leading eventually to spiritual and intellectual autonomy. And literary popularity had become the reading public's statement to the theologians, allowing a "filtering up" of attitudes and beliefs and doubtless a measure of influence over clerical authors. So not only does the printed word have the advantage of having survived from the seventeenth century when other forms of evidence have not; it was also becoming a most important medium of communication and direction in a time of social fragmentation, when laymen were becoming "articulate in the presence of the Deity" and even the arbiters of philosophical debate.[3]

Our evidence for the spiritual concerns and feelings of Englishmen, then, is in the books that they bought in largest numbers, whether sermons, devotional tracts, or theological treatises. And in

1. R. W., *Martine Mar-Sixtus* (London, 1591), sig. A3ᵛ.
2. [John Ball], *A Short Treatise Contayning all the Principall Grounds of Christian Religion*, 9th ed. (London, 1633), p. 165.
3. Louis B. Wright, *Middle-Class Culture in Elizabethan England* (Ithaca, N.Y., 1958), pp. 240–41.

excluding nonreligious literature we are excluding almost nothing which compares in popularity with these works.[4]

Beyond a choice of the evidence there was the problem of how to approach this evidence—whether to trust, in reading through the literature, to one's sensitivity to the authors' images and concerns, or to submit the books to a quantitative analysis which would show up the precise degree of attention to the various themes. At first it appeared that the repetitive nature of the literature would make a conventional description merely tedious, and that a quantitative analysis would be particularly appropriate to the conceptual level of the books: for their content was predictable enough for the question to be not so much what was mentioned, but how much space was devoted to each of the various well-worn themes. Viewing the evidence in a quantitative form made possible more direct comparisons between books in regard to certain philosophical, doctrinal, and social interests, revealing thought patterns of which even the authors may not have been aware. But there were other patterns and meanings which proved too elusive for a mechanical analysis. Attention to the authors' purposes and imagery gave a better feeling for their mentality than a quantification of content categories alone, so that another reading became necessary. And this may serve as a reminder that the justification of the study is not so much in its quantitative nature as in its concentration on books chosen for their popularity, and in the period chosen for·study.

The Seventeenth Century in English Cultural History

Among the things that could not be restored when Charles II returned to England were the philosophical assumptions of the period before the mid-century upheavals. The English mind had been unsettled as never before, and quite aside from the appearance of such giants in the history of thought as Hobbes, Newton, and Locke, there was something like a seismic disturbance in the very ground of discourse and scholarship. Radically new approaches to the study of nature, history, economics, politics, and society became possible.[5]

4. See my article, "On the Distribution of Religious and Occult Literature in Seventeenth-Century England," *The Library* 29 (1974):221–25.

5. John G. A. Pocock, *The Ancient Constitution and the Feudal Law* (Cambridge, 1957); William H. Greenleaf, *Order, Empiricism, and Politics* (London, 1964); R. H. Tawney, *Religion and the Rise of Capitalism* (1926; rpt. New York, 1947), pp. 152–53, 228–29; William L. Letwin, *The Origins of Scientific*

Only a generation separated Bacon, who advocated the claims of science against an overbearing religion, from Sir Thomas Browne, who pleaded the cause of religion in an age of science.[6] Besides certain changed ideas, then, there appears to have been a different mentality and awareness, and the modern problems of epistemology, subjectivity, and ideology have been traced to the seventeenth century.[7]

The new currents of thought are associated especially with the interregnum years of the 1640s and 1650s. Epicurean literature first appeared in England then, allied at first with an aristocratic ethos against the modernizing forces of science and Protestantism.[8] The beginnings of pornography in the same years have been interpreted as an Œdipal attack on social and religious authorities in the wake of the Puritan onslaught, and the appearance of the first criminal biographies at that time is open to the same interpretation.[9] Accusations of religious fanaticism or of cynical indifference during the period of the Civil War are said to have divorced the religious and secular impulses in English literature.[10]

Even before the Restoration there was evidence of a decline of religious interest and conviction.[11] Students of Restoration literature seldom fail to remark on such themes as the disappearance of religious preoccupations and supernatural sanctions, or the confrontation of "secular" characters with the religious and passive attitudes of the past.[12] And religious historians agree in characterizing it as

---

Economics (London, 1963); Herbert Butterfield, *The Origins of Modern Science, 1300–1800* (New York, 1965), p. 202.

6. Basil Willey, *The Seventeenth Century Background* (1935; rpt. Garden City, N.Y., 1953), p. 49.

7. Karl Mannheim, *Ideology and Utopia* (1929; rpt. New York, 1936), pp. 14–15, 61–62.

8. Thomas F. Mayo, *Epicurus in England (1650–1725)* (Dallas, 1934), pp. xi, 54–57, 78, 111.

9. David Foxon, *Libertine Literature in England, 1660–1745* (New Hyde Park, N.Y., 1965), pp. 47–51; Robert Singleton, "English Criminal Biography, 1651–1722," *Harvard Library Bulletin* 18 (1970):63–83.

10. Herbert J. C. Grierson, *Cross-Currents in Seventeenth-Century English Literature* (1929; rpt. New York, 1958), pp. ix–xvi.

11. Christopher Hill, *Intellectual Origins of the English Revolution* (Oxford, 1965), p. 118; Thomas Sprat, *History of the Royal Society* (1667; rpt. St. Louis, Mo., 1958), p. 340; W. K. Jordan, *The Development of Religious Toleration in England*, 4 vols. (Gloucester, Mass., 1965), 4:475–76; Grierson, *Cross-Currents*, p. 294; *The Diary of Ralph Thoresby*, ed. Joseph Hunter, 2 vols. (London, 1830), 1:57.

12. James Sutherland, *A Preface to Eighteenth-Century Poetry* (Oxford,

a pietistic age, in which a chastened religion took an introspective and private turn.

The present study does not challenge such a view. Indeed our constant theme will be the ways in which popular religious literature itself shows a decline of confidence, a contracting sphere for God's agency, and a lowering of affective tone. This is evident in the reduction of the variety of intellectual authorities cited to buttress doctrine, in a dwindling number of themes mentioned, and in a decline in religious dread. Authors seemed to fear an increasing presumptuousness as they looked about them at Restoration society. And religious partisans submerged their differences, feeling that religion itself was becoming isolated from the current of national life. All this does not necessarily mean a decline in the intensity with which religious beliefs were held. But a more private and spiritualized piety does mean a reduction in the public functions of religion.

For the Puritan party there were political as well as philosophical reasons for this "spiritualization" of religion. Its social and political goals had to be abandoned when the Stuarts and the Church of England were restored in 1660. The Puritans' particular millennial expectations had failed, God's purposes having proved even more inscrutable than they had supposed. The way was open for secular interpretations of history and politics.[13] Political expedience ensured that even the Anglican party was not restored to the position in the nation to which it aspired. There came a growing and painful awareness of the denominational character of the Church and of the extent of religious indifference, now that the Church's power was based more on belief than on the determination of the state to enforce adherence.[14]

But the changed status of religion resulted from social as well as political forces. In 1711 Addison summed up a development that had long been in process, when he expressed his hope of bringing

---

1948), p. 2; John Richetti, *Popular Fiction Before Richardson* (Oxford, 1969); D. P. Walker, *The Decline of Hell* (Chicago, 1964); cf. Patricia Meyer Spacks, *The Insistence of Horror: Aspects of the Supernatural in Eighteenth-Century Poetry* (Cambridge, Mass., 1962).

13. William Lamont, *Godly Rule; Politics and Religion, 1603–60* (London, 1969), pp. 163–86.

14. George Every, *The High Church Party, 1688–1718* (London, 1956), pp. xiii–xiv; James Fulton MacClear, "The Birth of the Free Church Tradition," *Church History* 26 (1957):99–131.

"philosophy out of closets and libraries, schools and colleges, to dwell in clubs and assemblies, at tea-tables and in coffee-houses."[15] Theology, too, was being made to prove itself in the pragmatic world of public opinion. New currents in philosophy were discrediting academic scholarship, and with the crisis of confidence in the intellectual and clerical elite, the authors were directing their appeals to the judgment of polite society. The invocation of "reason," of clear and distinct ideas, which is so prominent a feature of this period, is often an appeal to fashionable prejudice.[16] Appeals to reason may represent no more than a failure of argument, an impatience with traditions too difficult to master intellectually or refute. In such a period the pejorative "traditional" will be applied freely to those beliefs whose reasons have been forgotten. Whether this anti-intellectualism becomes confident and convincing depends partly on the internal inconsistencies or practical difficulties of the tradition under attack. But it depends also on the composition of the jury to which the appeal is directed. And in Restoration England the judgment on religious questions was falling in larger measure to the laity.

Partly, then, the changed appearance of Restoration religious thought may only reflect a change in the social groups which command the historian's attention. No doubt the dislocations of the Interregnum made Englishmen more conscious of popular undercurrents and of the relativity of religious outlook, but the most profound change may be in whose beliefs seemed important. And when an intellectual elite is displaced in this way, one would expect just such a narrowing of the concept of reason and simplification of intellectual life as have been noted.[17]

One would also expect changes in terminology. Ian Ramsey has seen the generation of John Locke as the first to take the language of the Bible as plain and unequivocal prose, raising logical difficulties that had not been important so long as the response to that language was affective and spiritual.[18] A study of theological book

15. Joseph Addison, *The Spectator*, no. 10 (1711).

16. Mark Pattison, *Essays by the late Mark Pattison*, ed. Henry Nettleship, 2 vols. (Oxford, 1889), 2:68–80, 53; see also Christopher Hill, "'Reason' and 'Reasonableness' in seventeenth-century England," *British Journal of Sociology* 20 (1969):235–52.

17. G. R. Cragg, *From Puritanism to the Age of Reason* (Cambridge, 1966), pp. 225–28; S. L. Bethell, *The Cultural Revolution of the Seventeenth Century* (London, 1951), pp. 34–36, 57, 65.

18. *Religious Language* (New York, 1963), p. 107.

titles indicates a shift in the understanding of religion reflecting the transition from a personalistic to an objectified world view. It was in the seventeenth century that these titles abandoned the term *faith*, indicating a whole dimension of life and consciousness, for *religion*, denoting an explanation of life or a set of propositions. Englishmen began to speak of religions in the plural for the first time and to distinguish between natural and revealed religion. It only remained to the eighteenth century to complete the transition from "religion" to an emphasis specifically on "Christianity."[19] Even when the terms used in theological discourse remained the same they might change their meaning and "demythologize" religious concepts. This might be done without alarming readers as Samuel Clarke and other liberals did when they offered to change the language of theology itself.[20]

Underlying even these semantic changes, there is the question of the effect of print itself on the religious mentality. The committing of doctrine and spiritual direction to print has itself been taken as an element in the secularization of English culture. Religion in a relatively "oral" society has a flexibility which allows it to adjust to other cultural values and to keep conflicts from becoming glaringly apparent. Print, on the other hand, hardens distinctions and encourages division. In order for any society to cohere despite such disagreement over ultimate questions it must segregate religion from its other values or institutions. And this is precisely one definition of secularization—the divorce of various aspects of life and thought from religious or at least ecclesiastical direction. While this understanding of secularity does not necessarily imply a decline in religious beliefs, their differentiation and isolation from former social and cultural supports is likely to lead to such a decline. And print aids this process too, by making beliefs more explicit and more self-conscious and hence more open to doubt and attack. The very permanence of print hastens intellectual change and stimulates that addiction to novelty that is a feature of secularity.[21]

19. Wilfred Cantwell Smith, *The Meaning and End of Religion* (New York, 1962), pp. 31–45, 74–77.

20. H. L. Short, "The Later History of the English Presbyterians," *The Hibbert Journal* 64 (1966):129–32; Willey, *Seventeenth Century Background*, pp. 150–54.

21. Elizabeth L. Eisenstein, "Some Conjectures about the Impact of Printing on Western Society and Thought," *Journal of Modern History* 40 (1968):25–42, 53; Jack Goody, ed., *Literacy in Traditional Societies* (Cambridge, 1968), pp. 2–3, 67, 312; Walter J. Ong, *The Presence of the Word* (New Haven, 1967), pp. 10–16, 162–63.

In short, the period of the Restoration appears to be one of intellectual and even psychological transformation, in which religion underwent profound changes if not decline. The year 1660 was the beginning of a new era, in which the hope of religious uniformity was finally relinquished by the English government and freedom of conscience, though not of worship, was tacitly recognized. The survival of Dissent depended in large part on the encouragement of its literary tradition, and therefore on the publishing industry. And the Church, too, was searching for new foundations in popular opinion rather than in political might, and was producing a specifically Anglican devotional and apologetical literature to that end.

But it should also be remembered that England underwent a remarkable religious revival in the next two centuries, so that the period 1660–1711 may be seen as falling between two periods of religious assertiveness. We may, therefore, interpret our picture of the popular religious mentality as one of concentration and conservation of energies as much as one of defensiveness. To be sure, this period in England's history has been characterized as unassertive in a very general sense. Christopher Hill thought that he noticed a certain timidity in the generation after 1614.[22] And in a study of achievement-related ideals in several types of literature of the period between 1400 and 1830, the late seventeenth century showed the weakest orientation toward mastery or independence, while the beginnings of Puritanism and of Methodism were coincidental with high achievement orientation.[23] As J. H. Hexter has pointed out, there is no law of the "conservation of historical energy" by which an increase in secular dynamism must necessarily be compensated or caused by a decrease in religious energy.[24] The contraction of confidence and the spirit of retrenchment characteristic of the religious life of this period can be detected in other areas of England's cultural life. The desire on the part of Deist and orthodox Christian alike to simplify doctrine and to reduce religious practice to its essentials finds its counterpart in the reductionism of the physics and the psychology of the time. This impulse may have owed more to a wish to transcend old controversies and establish an agreed basis for discussion than to the arrogance of a more secular philosophy.

22. Hill, *Intellectual Origins*, pp. 11, 95, 221, 299.
23. David McClelland, *The Achieving Society* (Princeton, 1961), pp. 132–49.
24. *Reappraisals in History* (London, 1961), pp. 40–42.

The Choice of Books

In the seventeenth century the number of editions a book enjoyed was a good indication of its popularity, since editions were of certain standard sizes. Since the sixteenth century the Stationers' Company of London, with one of the most effective monopolies of any English industry, had set limits to the press runs of editions.[25] The type was then to be redistributed, making the demand for compositors more constant. By the company's orders of 1635, type larger than brevier was to be redistributed after an impression or edition of 1,500 or 2,000 copies. On petition, the Master and Wardens might allow 3,000, and that number was routinely allowed for brevier, and 5,000 for nonpareil—unusually small typefaces. Special patents not subject to these regulations were granted, but only for the printing of Bibles, Psalters, Prayer Books, schoolbooks (including the authorized catechisms), and almanacs.[26] Since the demand for these books was not expected to be sensitive to currents of opinion, they were not considered in this study.

The lapse of the Licensing Act in 1695 meant the end of the Stationers' monopoly, but the maximum limits on impressions remained standard until the nineteenth century. Even earlier it had not been usual to produce at the limit; two members of the company had argued in 1652 over whether 1,500 copies was an abnormally large edition or not.[27] The run for learned books was often only 500. First editions of most kinds of literature were on the small side—750 or 1,000—but reprints were larger as a matter of course.[28] The more editions a work had formerly sold, the larger the subsequent press-runs, compounding the importance of those books which could show

25. H. S. Bennett, *English Books and Readers, 1558 to 1603* (Cambridge, 1965), p. 58; Cyprian Blagden, *The Stationers' Company* (Cambridge, Mass., 1960), pp. 28, 45, 124.

26. Edward Arber, ed., *A Transcript of the Registers of the Company of Stationers of London 1554–1640,* 5 vols. (London and Birmingham, 1875–94), 4:21–22. Judging from *Printing Patents; Abridgements of Patent Specifications Relating to Printing, 1617–1857* (London, 1859), there were almost no special patents issued to exempt particular titles from these regulations after 1623, and those few also concerned schoolbooks.

27. Richard D. Altick, *The English Common Reader: A Social History of the Mass Reading Public 1800–1900* (Chicago, 1957), p. 20.

28. John Johnson and Strickland Gibson, "Print and Privilege at Oxford to the Year 1700," *Oxford Bibliographical Society; Publications* 7 (1941–42):123, 147; D. F. McKenzie, *The Cambridge University Press, 1696–1712. A Bibliographical Study,* 2 vols. (Cambridge, 1966), 1:99–101.

the largest number of editions. In the eighteenth century, when it was possible to print new editions from standing type, the usual edition was still around 1,000 copies, with 2,000 considered very large. It is often commented that sermons had among the largest runs in that century, with subsequent editions numbering 2,000 or even 3,000.[29] But as late as 1800 an edition of 1,000 copies of most forms of literature was still considered a large one.[30]

It is clear that religious best sellers were printed in the largest editions known to the industry, usually 2,000 or 3,000. Two religious works that enjoyed a modest popularity, though not enough to place them among our best sellers, claimed to have sold 10,000 copies when, in each case, we can account for about six editions.[31] Sir Roger L'Estrange, the Crown's Surveyor of the Press, calculated that ten or twelve impressions of a religious work meant about 30,000 copies.[32] The nineteenth edition of John Rawlet's *Christian Monitor* advertised 95,000 copies sold, and Defoe's *True-Born Englishman* is reported to have sold 80,000 copies in perhaps twenty-one editions.[33] In November 1678, Sir John Verney sent his father sermons by Tillotson and Stillingfleet which were occasioned by the revelation of the Popish Plot. "The last only came out yesterday, and before night the whole impression of 4000 was sold, and this day will be a second Impression of 3000," he wrote.[34] Ordinary devotional

29. Fredson Bowers, *Principles of Bibliographical Description* (New York, 1962), p. 312; Ivor W. J. Machin, "Popular Religious Works of the Eighteenth Century: Their Vogue and Influence" (Ph.D. diss., University of London, 1939), p. 327; Robert D. Harlan, "Some Additional Figures of Distribution of Eighteenth-Century English Books," *Papers of the Bibliographical Society of America* 59 (1965):160–70; Patricia Hernlund, "William Strahan's Ledgers: Standard Charges for Printing, 1738–1785," *Studies in Bibliography* 20 (1967):104–10.

30. Marjorie Plant, *The English Book Trade*, 2d ed. (London, 1965), pp. 404, 412; Richard D. Altick, "Nineteenth-Century English Best-Sellers: A Further List," *Studies in Bibliography* 22 (1969):198.

31. R. E. [i.e., Edward Fowler], *A Scripture Catechism*, see Edward Arber, ed., *The Term Catalogues, 1668–1709 A.D.; With a Number for Easter Term, 1711 A.D.*, 3 vols. (London, 1903–6), 3:86; Robert Nelson, *A Companion for the Festivals and Fasts*, see *Dictionary of National Biography*, 40:212.

32. Henry R. Plomer, *A Short History of English Printing, 1476–1900* (London, 1927), p. 170.

33. See S. Manship's advertisement in John Norris, *Treatises upon Several Subjects* (London, 1697), sig. A7ᵛ. Alexandre Beljame, *Men of Letters and the English Public in the Eighteenth Century 1660–1744* (London, 1948), p. 309.

34. Margaret Maria Lady Verney, *Verney Letters of the Eighteenth Century from the MSS. at Clayton House*, 2 vols. (London, 1930), 1:365. I owe this reference to Dr. Henry Horwitz.

literature would not have enjoyed such a sensational first sale, but it sometimes sold more than the five or six editions recorded for these two political sermons.

There are two independent sources of information as to the numbers of editions for this period, Donald Wing's *Short-Title Catalogue* of all English books from the period 1641–1700 which have survived to the present, and the less complete listings in the *Term Catalogues* (1668–1711), a quarterly compilation by London booksellers advertising their new stock.[35] The lapse of these catalogues provided a terminal date for the study, although the year 1711 also marked the surge of Tory concern for the Church and changes in the activity of the Society for Promoting Christian Knowledge which affected religious publishing (see chapter 2).

As to the question of what contemporaries considered to be religious literature, the Term Catalogues and other trade catalogues all gave "Divinity" sections pride of place in their listings. There are few surprises; Marcus Aurelius might turn up in a section on divinity, but philosophical treatises and collections of moral epigrams appeared in other sections, variously labeled, even when

35. Donald Wing, *Short-Title Catalogue of Books Printed in England, Scotland, Ireland, Wales, and British America and of English Books Printed in Other Countries, 1641–1700*, 3 vols. (New York, 1945); supplemented by idem, *A Gallery of Ghosts* (New York, 1967); Edwin Wolf, *A Check-List of the Books in the Library Company of Philadelphia in and supplementary to Wing's Short-Title Catalogue 1641–1700* (Philadelphia, 1959); W. G. Hiscock, *The Christ Church Supplement to Wing's Short-Title Catalogue, 1641–1700* (Oxford, 1956); Godfrey Davies and Mary Isabel Fry, "Supplements to the *Short-Title Catalogue, 1641–1700*," *Huntington Library Quarterly* 16 (1953):393–436; John Alden, *Bibliographia Hibernica: Additions and Corrections to Wing* (Charlottesville, Va., 1955); idem, *Wing Addenda and Corrigenda* (Charlottesville, Va., 1958); W. J. Cameron, *A Short-Title Catalogue of Books Printed in Britain and British Books Printed Abroad 1641–1700 Held in Australian Libraries* (Sydney, 1962); A. H. Hall, *A List of Books Printed in the British Isles and of English Books Printed Abroad Before 1701 in Guildhall Library*, 2 vols. (London, 1966–67); Cyprian Blagden, "The Missing Term Catalogue," *Studies in Bibliography* 7 (1955):185–90. These supplements yielded meagre results. More helpful, especially for the years between 1700 and 1711, was the *British Museum Catalogue of Printed Books*. Other supplements were [G. R. Barnes], *A List of Books printed in Cambridge at The University Press, 1521–1800* (Cambridge, 1935); McKenzie, *Cambridge University Press*; Falconer Madan, *Oxford Books; a Bibliography of Printed Works Relating to the University and City of Oxford or Printed or Published There*, 3 vols. (Oxford, 1931); Joseph Smith, *A Descriptive Catalogue of Friends' Books*, 2 vols. (London, 1867); W. T. Whitley, *A Baptist Bibliography*, 2 vols. (London, 1916); Charles Evans, *American Bibliography*, 12 vols. (New York, 1941–42); *Catalogus Librorum Impressorum Bibliothecae Bodleianae*, 3 vols. (Oxford, 1843).

their content concerned religious questions. Ecclesiastical controversy might sometimes be found under "Miscellanies," church history was ordinarily under "History," and devotional poetry appeared in a "Poetry" section. And, while such works were not excluded from our consideration because they were not labelled "divinity" by contemporaries, in fact their popularity was never such as to challenge the more ordinary works of religious direction.

While the estimate of popularity was based on the number of editions traced for each book, it cannot be assumed that editions were correctly numbered. Pirated editions might repeat the number of a legitimate edition. Or the number might be inflated for promotional reasons, on a new title page which only disguised a reissue of older sheets.[36] But it is reasonable to assume that this tactic was reserved for books whose sale was lagging and would not affect the works chosen for this study, whose popularity is unquestionable. On the other hand, it is important not to discount an edition number simply because there are no known copies bearing the numbers of earlier editions. For it is clear that many whole editions have vanished and numerous others are now known by a single copy. This seems especially true of the most popular works, including schoolbooks, which were seldom bound or protected in libraries and were simply read to pieces.

In the estimate of relative popularity, only editions dated from 1660 to 1711 were counted. This eliminated several books which had formerly experienced a comparable popularity.[37] The seventeenth-century book market was very much subject to the vicissitudes of demand, and the failure of popularity shown by a fall in sales was taken as more significant than any lingering influence that remaining copies no doubt still exercised.

The titles which showed the greatest number of editions fell into three groups: those whose popularity extended through the whole of our period, those popular mostly before 1688—when the Revolution, the Toleration Act, and the end of the Licensers' censorship (1695) make a natural break—and those popular mostly after 1689. The eighteen leading books from the first group were chosen, hav-

36. Bowers, *Principles of Bibliographical Description*, pp. 41, 66–67; Marc Eccles, "A Survey of Elizabethan Reading," *Huntington Library Quarterly* 5 (1942):180–82, counts editions to establish popularity, but does not discount some which he takes to be "mere variants."

37. H. S. Bennett, *English Books and Readers, 1603 to 1640* (Cambridge, 1970), pp. 93, 101, 213.

ing fifteen or more editions each. The nine top books from the group with an early popularity had all enjoyed thirteen or more editions concentrated in a much shorter span of time.[38] This group is of interest not only because of their initial popularity, but also because they fell from favor in the course of the period. The ten leading books from the later period had seven editions or more, in some cases fewer editions than certain books which were excluded from the first group. Still, if one considers the shorter time of sale of these later works (none of them written before 1686), the frequency of their reprinting does make them comparable in popularity to those included in that group. Having this later group helped us to avoid a bias toward older works which had a longer period of sale, and allowed an examination of shifts in interest from the earlier to the latter half of the period.

We may here anticipate the objection that some books have an influence out of proportion to their sale, an argument which might be used to justify a concentration on those books which still have an intrinsic interest. Even when ideas do seep downward through the levels of culture in the manner envisioned in this objection, the only measure of the extent of this influence is the popularity of these works or others derived from them. It would seem, for example, that Henry Hammond was just such a divine's divine, inspiring the works of Richard Allestree and other popular authors. His own *Practical Catechism*, however, was not sufficiently popular to be included among our best sellers, although the works of some of his admirers were. Still, if these derivative works were analyzed, one might find that some of his most characteristic and interesting ideas had not filtered down to the more popular literature. And it will become apparent that many of the theological enthusiasms of prominent Restoration divines were not shared by the reading public. Indeed, the present study was designed to screen out those interests which were confined to the clergy and to investigate the audience more than the authors. It is an inquiry into the social more than the intellectual side of religious history.

Naturally, the number of books to be analyzed might have been larger. But beyond the desire to keep the project within manageable bounds it was considered important not to dilute the results of a study of these books with data from works which were not

38. Counted as one of the early best sellers was a group of John Hart's six most popular tracts. See chapter 3.

comparable in popularity. In all three groups, each cutoff point came at a natural break, after a popular work that ran to several more editions than the work following it, or, in the case of the first group, before a number of works virtually tied at the next level of edition numbers. To have included all of these works would have clouded the results, for together they would almost have counter-balanced the works which were chosen, many of which had a marked superiority in sales. One might have weighted the books according to the number of their editions when it came to assessing their interests quantitatively, in hopes of getting the truest picture of the popular mind. But this would have raised the question of whether to weight those written late in the period more heavily to counter the advantage of those with a longer sale time. It would also have magnified the uncertainties over the exact number or size of these editions, and the effect of free distribution or lending of the books, a problem discussed in chapter 2. And the study would have become a comparison, not of books at all, but rather of artificial units of literary evidence. Our initial intent, however, is a descrip-tion of the best sellers, so that any who would decline the inference that they represent the popular religious mentality of the age may yet find the description useful for its picture of those books. But surely these books are the most valid evidence we have for the popular mind of that remote period. And beyond that, our method of analysis might stand comparison with modern polls, which often create the opinion they measure by raising unreal questions and suggesting and limiting responses.

As it happened, there were twenty works by recognizably Angli-can authors and thirteen by Puritans or Dissenters, that is, men who sought the reorganization of the Church of England or who were actually cast out for nonconformity. Comparisons among the books could thus be made along the lines of party affiliation. And three other groups of books were chosen for a similar analysis and com-parison, by Catholic, Quaker, and notoriously "Liberal" authors of the same period.[39] The works chosen to represent the Liberal posi-

---

39. By Catholics: [Henry Turberville], *An Abridgment of Christian Doc-trine* (Douai, 1661); [Theophilus Dorrington], *Reform'd Devotions, in Medi-tations, Hymns, and Petitions*, 4th ed. (London, 1696), a mildly Protestant ver-sion, and the most popular form, of John Austin's *Devotions in the Antient Way of Offices*; Robert Parsons, *A Christian Directorie* (n.p., 1585); Jeremias Drexel, *The Considerations of Drexelius Upon Eternitie* (London, 1654); Francis de Sales, *Introduction to the Devout Life* (1609; rpt. New York, 1966). By Quak-

tion were widely condemned in their own day, for threatening the
very basis of revealed religion. In order to provide the most direct
comparisons with our best sellers, the books in these groups had to
be works written for a popular audience, presenting a positive declaration of their own position rather than a satirical treatment of their
opponents. Of the available books, choice was again made on the
basis of popularity.

The Form of the Analysis

In the 1740s some Swedish Lutheran clergymen attempted to discredit a new Pietist hymnbook by comparing its emphases and
expressions with those of Scripture, their confessions, and older
hymnals. They thought they would make their points more con-
vincingly by an actual count of the images and doctrines used, and
thus "content analysis" was born.[40] There are now so many methods
known by that name, some of them not quantitative, that it has
become necessary to describe just what is attempted in a particular
study.

In dealing with more than fifty books, it would be quite unsatisfactory to depend on one's impressions of the drift of the literature.
No matter how much sympathy the historian brings to the study,
he cannot be sure that what strikes him does not represent individual and anachronistic interests. And so, as a corrective, it seemed
advisable to submit the literature to a rigorously quantitative analysis which could give each paragraph due weight. In this way the
study became an investigation as much of religious behavior as of

---

ers: William Penn, *No Cross, No Crown* (1669; rpt. Philadelphia, 1845), as
well as his *A Key, opening the Way*, also included among the best sellers; Robert Barclay, *A Catechism and Confession of Faith* (1673; rpt. Philadelphia,
1726); Edward Burrough, *A Declaration to all the World of Our Faith, and
what we Believe* (London, 1657); James Nayler, *Love to the Lost* (1656; rpt.
Cincinnati, 1829); three tracts by George Fox, taken together, *To all that would
know the Way to the Kingdom* (London, 1706), *What the unchangeable God
is* (n.p., 1685), and *An Epistle to all Professors in New-England, Germany, and
other Parts of the called Christian World* (n.p., 1673). By Liberals: John
Biddle, *A Confession of Faith Touching the Holy Trinity* (London, 1648);
[Herbert Croft], *The Naked Truth* (n.p., 1675); John Locke, *The Reasonable-
ness of Christianity* (1695; rpt. Chicago, 1965); Stephen Nye, *A Discourse
Concerning Natural and Revealed Religion* (London, 1696); John Toland,
Christianity not Mysterious, 2d ed. (London, 1696).

40. Karin Dovring, "Quantitative Semantics in 18th Century Sweden," *Public Opinion Quarterly* 18 (1954–55):389–94.

religious thought, since it deals with what contemporaries wrote *about* more than with what they said. It later seemed necessary to read the books again with an eye to their purpose and argument, as well as content. But the conventional nature of the content did lend itself to a quantitative analysis, the ideas being so commonplace that the initial question was the frequency of mention of the various themes.

For the purpose of the quantitative analysis, a list of subject categories was devised to represent the themes which engaged the authors—matters of intellectual authority, religious doctrine, and social attitude.[41] These categories are listed in the appendix, and referred to in the text by number. From each paragraph in the books, the two most prominent subjects were "coded" or recorded, with indication of negative attitudes when appropriate.[42] This seemed the most natural approach to the literature, since the paragraph is the unit of thought and is normally used to bring two or more themes together. In testing various methods, it became apparent that to settle on only one dominant theme per paragraph would not give a true or "valid" representation of the literature. Too much would go unrecorded. On the other hand, to mark every slightest

41. Louis Schneider and Sanford M. Dornbusch, *Popular Religion: Inspirational Books in America* (Chicago, 1958), have developed the most inclusive list of religious content categories, but because they were in functionalist terms they may have given the resulting picture of religion its functionalist cast. A third of the paragraphs in the books they studied could not be coded according to their categories (pp. 169–70), indicating that some of the concerns of the literature were ignored. Labeling our categories in the language of the authors rather than of the social sciences also made the coding less a matter of judgment and therefore probably more reliable.

42. Operational definitions of the categories, coding directions and permissible variations are included with the results of the coding in my dissertation, "Popular Religious Literature in England, 1660–1711: A Content Analysis" (University of Iowa, 1970), Appendix B. Variations necessary because of the special character of individual books appear there in Appendix A. The reliability of the coding was satisfactory when the results for whole books were compared, although the treatment of individual categories by different coders was sometimes doubtful. Checks by a nonexperienced coder found agreement of 75%, 76%, 89%, and 83%, on four books chosen at random (figured at twice the number of agreements by the two coders, divided by the sum of the marks of both coders). Checks by my own recoding after several months were nearly the same: 85%, 74%, 78.5%, and 84.5%. The more general categories proved least reliable, and these were the categories that were most easily combined into the clusters or typologies. And reliability for these typologies was higher than that for a book taken as a whole, seldom falling below 90%. This indicates that the variation in coding was due to some overlapping in the categories, more than to judgments as to which were the primary themes of the paragraph.

mention of any of our categories would have raised the problem of the "reliability" of the coding, which is determined by comparison with an independent coding of the same material. Unless the coder was restricted to the more prominent themes in each paragraph, an endless search for underlying attitudes and implied concepts would have increased the possibility of disagreements among coders. It might also have been less true to the way that contemporaries read the literature. And it would have been impossible to keep all the categories in mind to catch every whisper of a theme. Memory was not involved when the most apparent themes were first decided upon and then matched on the category list. The length of the list then became an advantage, since it was easier to find an exact match and less often necessary to translate the content into a more general attitudinal category. After the coding was complete, it was possible to combine and recombine the individual categories into clusters representing more general interests or into "typologies" contrasting different religious temperaments.

In description of the content of the books, the number of times a theme was mentioned is often less meaningful than the percentage of the total paragraphs which was devoted to it—its frequency. The books varied considerably in length, so that six mentions might represent a major theme in one book but be almost lost in a longer one. When the books were grouped together for comparison of those popular in different periods or those from different camps, these frequencies could be averaged to produce the group means given in the appendix. Statistical tests were applied to the comparisons where the reliability of the data was firmest, that is, when groups of books were compared in relation to the clusters of categories. We also tested correlations between different categories or types for significance, using the data only from the best sellers and not from the books by Catholic, Quaker, or Liberal authors.[43]

43. F-ratio and t-tests were used to see whether variation within the groups was small enough for the variation between group means to be significant. In other words, the tests were to see how great was the chance that the different group means might nevertheless have come from a common "population." If that chance was less than .05, it is termed a "significant" difference. For the correlation of categories or typologies, Spearman rho rank-order coefficients were calculated and tested for significance at the .05 level. Tests of correlation were done after the dissertation was completed, and so the correlations reported here supersede those calculated in the dissertation. The Spearman coefficients are reported in my article, "Religious Typologies and Popular Religion in Restoration England," Church History 45 (1976):32–41. Correlations and t-tests

The primary purpose of the study is descriptive, to provide a profile of the religious literature of England at a time of significant change. The very absence of a governing hypothesis has reduced the chance of bias in the coding. But the wide range of categories allows us to test various observations and implicit hypotheses concerning the popular religious mind of the time, or more general typologies of religiousness characteristic of any time.

The most obvious such typology used of our period is that of Anglican and Dissenter, which has connoted differences in behavior and outlook far beyond the quarrel over church order. During the seventeenth century, some began to see the distinction between authoritarian and rationalist as more important. This, in turn, has given way to the religious typologies defined by Troeltsch (church and sect), Weber (traditional and prophetic), and William James (healthy- and sick-minded). For the present study these typologies have been constructed from those categories which seem most relevant, as listed in footnotes at the appropriate point. All such typologies have at times been used for purposes of advocacy, as were the ancient distinctions of elect and unregenerate, confessor and infidel, and orthodox and heretic, answering the concerns of different periods. The safest approach may be to remind oneself of the various typologies that have been proposed so that their artificiality is fully in view. And their comparative success in describing the issues of this period can be assessed.

In reference to philosophical basis the familiar distinctions are between authoritarian and liberal positions, and between Old- and New-Testament biases. In chapter 4 the usefulness of these typologies will be tested and any significant differences between the groups of books or significant correlations with other typologies reported. Chapter 5 will deal with the degree of emphasis on God and on Christ, and with the image of God as stern and unpredictable or benign and restrained. Related to these subjects are the

---

significant at the .01 level are listed in that article. Factor analysis was not attempted with the typologies, since they overlapped in composition, or with the categories, because there were too many of them in relation to the number of books. One caution should be observed in the use of these data. For single categories a percentage figure indicates the percentage of paragraphs devoted to the theme. But when the percentages for different categories are combined this is no longer the case, since, frequently, both categories may have been coded from the same paragraphs. The most one can say is that the added total represents that percentage of the total codings, which was about 1.8 times the number of paragraphs.

contrasts between an emphasis on the supernatural and grace as opposed to nature, and between a "religious authoritarianism," expressing mortification or awe and a melioristic world view suggesting a comfortable relationship with God. Chapter 6 will be concerned with concentration on man or self, a conversionist as opposed to a moralistic view of religious experience, evidence of anxiety or restrictiveness as opposed to confidence or generosity, and a passive or contemplative mentality as against an active or engaged one. In chapter 7, interest will focus on the degree of concentration on society or the church, a social authoritarianism as against social liberalism or openness to change, a "churchly" allegiance as opposed to sectarian alienation, "traditionalism" as against a "prophetic" stance toward culture, and a priestly and sacramental as opposed to an evangelical and ethical approach to religion. In chapter 8, the question of a general authoritarianism or liberalism will be explored, and also the relative success of these typologies in describing the religious issues or mentalities of the late seventeenth century.

But it is possible that the most obvious disagreements among the books refer to debates that already belonged to the past. As Zevedei Barbu has observed, "It is often a feeling which is dying in the hearts of men that reverberates vigorously in their cultural products."[44] When it comes to identifying the interests and conflicts that were only then emerging, it may be particularly the individual categories, and even the turns of phrase, that will seem most important.

44. *Problems of Historical Psychology* (New York, 1960), pp. 52–53.

2. The Reading Public in
Restoration England

The late Helen White, commenting on the Elizabethan age, re-marked on a growing consciousness among religious writers of the needs of various elements in the population besides the usual cleri-cal audience. The relative cheapness of printed literature had ex-panded the audience for religious works to the point that, by 1550, books were addressed specifically to householders and even ser-vants.[1] According to some estimates of late-medieval literacy, the market for such literature had existed for some time. Although Sir Thomas More may have been exaggerating in his guess that half the English nation could read, in 1543 the government acknowl-edged the danger he had foreseen and forbade the reading of the English Bible by women, artificers, apprentices, journeymen, serv-ing men, husbandmen and laborers, as conducive to controversy and radicalism.[2] What evidence can be gathered suggests that by the mid–seventeenth century a third of the adult male population in England could read, with the figure for London perhaps as high as a half.[3]

It is possible that literacy declined after the intellectual excite-ment of the Interregnum, as educational opportunities shrank.[4]

1. Helen C. White, *The Tudor Books of Private Devotion* (Madison, Wis., 1951), pp. 156, 167–68, 241–42.

2. J. W. Adamson, "The Extent of Literacy in England in the Fifteenth and Sixteenth Centuries: Notes and Conjectures," *The Library*, 4th ser. 10 (1929): 167–73.

3. Lawrence Stone, "The Educational Revolution in England, 1560–1640," *Past and Present* 28 (1964):42–43; Peter Laslett, *The World We Have Lost* (New York, 1965), pp. 194–98.

4. Altick, *English Common Reader*, pp. 30–32; cf. Lawrence Stone, "Lit-eracy and Education in England, 1640–1900," *Past and Present* 42 (1969): 69–139.

Book prices, which had risen in the 1630s, rose again in the early eighteenth century and have been estimated at ten times more of the average wage than would be the case today.[5] But we need not imagine that because by Gregory King's contemporary estimates half of all Englishmen were below the line of economic dependence, or because only a fifth or a tenth of all wills mentioned books, that most were without anything to read.[6] If the prices of our best-selling religious books are an indication of their availability, one would expect a very wide distribution. Prices for most of them are known, and the lowest ones advertised ranged from two pence to five shillings.[7] The average was around one shilling, and nearly all (85 per cent) cost eighteen pence or less. Some prices recorded in *Bibliotheca Annua* for 1699–1703 were twice those for the same books in Robert Clavell's 1674 catalogue, but others were less. When Clavell gave up listing prices in 1680 it was not because of a general inflation but because of the sensitivity of prices to popularity.[8] A recent study of Bible production indicates availability well down into the laboring classes.[9] Of course, on those who were literate the few books they had must have made a vivid impression, and in those more thrifty days a single book must have found a wide readership.[10] Authors sometimes recommended reading aloud to those who were unable to read for themselves, which "in our days are but few, blessed be God, in comparison with former ages."[11] And some books were specifically directed to the poor: *The Whole Duty of Man* was addressed to "the meanest reader" and avoided discus-

5. Altick, *English Common Reader*, pp. 22–23; Ian Watt, *The Rise of the Novel* (Berkeley, 1957), pp. 41–46.
   6. Ibid., p. 40; Laslett, *World We Have Lost*, p. 196; Thomas Kelly, *Early Public Libraries* (London, 1966), p. 27.
   7. Prices were taken from the *Term Catalogues, Bibliotheca Annua*, comps. A. Roper and W. Turner, 2 vols. (1699–1704; rpt. London, 1964), and Robert Clavell, *A Catalogue of all the Books printed in England since the Dreadful Fire of London*, 4 vols. (1672–96; rpt. Farnborough, Hants., 1965).
   8. Ibid., 3: "To the Reader."
   9. "On the Distribution of Religious and Occult Literature," pp. 221–25. See David Cressy, "Literacy in Pre-Industrial England," *Societas* 4 (1974): 229–40, for a breakdown of literacy by class.
   10. See E. S. Chalk, "Circulation of XVIII-Century Newspapers," *Notes and Queries* 169 (1935):336.
   11. Richard Baxter, *A Call to the Unconverted*, in *The Practical Works of Richard Baxter*, 4 vols. (London, 1854), 2:538; Symon [or Simon] Patrick, *A Book for Beginners*, in *The Works of Symon Patrick, D.D.*, ed. Rev. Alexander Taylor, 9 vols. (Oxford, 1858), 1:623.

sion, for instance, of the duties of magistrates, "none of that rank being like to read this treatise."[12]

One of our popular authors, John Rawlet, suggested that his threepenny book be given away, and claimed that he was urged to publish by "some pious Persons, both of City and Country, who intend to give some of them away to poor People about them."[13] Richard Baxter advertised his work as suitable for "the richer sort, that have any pity on such miserable souls, to give to the unsanctified that need them (if they have not fitter at hand to use and give)."[14] Several others of the books were advertised as cheaper by the hundred, and one that recommended itself as "proper to be given at Funerals" had a large sale.[15] Some books of the period had as a suggestive part of their titles "A New Year's Gift," and several of these were religious books. And there is evidence that clergymen and teachers, especially, privately distributed Bibles, Rawlet's *Christian Monitor*, and *The Whole Duty of Man* to the poor, as well as other works which—like the various "New Year's Gifts"—did not achieve any real popularity.[16] Rawlet envisioned more systematic schemes of book distribution, calculating that only five shillings could supply a home with a Bible, a Prayer Book, and *The Whole Duty of Man*, and asked "rich Landlords and Gentlemen" to put poor children out to school and give them Bibles at least.[17]

Plans such as these were eventually put in motion by Rawlet's friend and biographer, Thomas Bray, as part of the work of the Society for Promoting Christian Knowledge. It became such a favorite form of charity in the eighteenth century that the activity of the S.P.C.K. alone would make it difficult to use reprinting as an index of popular preference. One might merely be studying the ideology which these "rich Landlords and Gentlemen" were attempting to inculcate in their dependents. But it is doubtful that any books were made best sellers by promotion before 1711. Rather, it seems that social and religious leaders, and certainly the S.P.C.K., promoted books that had already demonstrated their popularity. Until 1711

12. [Richard Allestree], *The Whole Duty of Man* (London, 1677), p. 291.
13. *Christian Monitor* 25th ed. (Boston, 1733), p. 2.
14. Baxter, *Call to the Unconverted*, p. 501.
15. Edward Pearse, *The Great Concern*, 21st ed. (Boston, 1705).
16. F. H. West, "A Nottinghamshire Parson in the 17th Century," *Church Quarterly Review* 151 (1950):8; *DNB*, 31:80; 53:264; *Diary of Ralph Thoresby*, 1:195–96, 215.
17. Rawlet, *Christian Monitor*, pp. 60–61.

the resources of the S.P.C.K. were spent in distributing books which were not in competition with those considered here—Bibles, Prayer Books, and Welsh translations.[18]

It is true that seventeenth-century authors commonly directed their books to an audience of substantial, or at least middling, families. Two of the earliest works were addressed to "godly Householders," and confronted problems such as overeating, making wills, and managing alms, which seem remote from the condition of the poor.[19] Others dealt briefly with the concerns of magistrates, ministers, and masters of families.[20] So we might, in any case, describe this as a literature for the more prosperous classes. But most of the popular works were written for a very general audience, and some specifically recognized the needs of several stations in society. One which was dedicated to the future Queen Mary contained a section of shorter prayers for the use of servants.[21] Jeremy Taylor addressed himself to rich and poor alike,[22] and those works which were directed to young people and servants were not noticeably simpler in expression.

Authors were sometimes poor judges of the appeal of their books; a copy of the humble *Whole Duty of Man* found its way into the library of the Duke of Ormonde, and the book figured in the famous squabble between Queen Anne and the Duchess of Marlborough.[23] The works which had originally been addressed to lawyers and gentlemen could never have become best sellers if their audience had been limited to those groups.[24] Conversely, the rich may have taken more kindly to Rawlet's book than its ostensible audience of

18. John S. Simon, *John Wesley and the Religious Societies*, 2d ed. (London, 1955), p. 21; Kelly, *Early Public Libraries*, pp. 106–14.

19. Ball, *A Short Treatise*, "To the Reader"; Lewis Bayly, *The Practice of Piety*, 38th ed. (London, 1637), pp. 289, 383, 547, 406, 438.

20. Pearse, *Great Concern*, pp. 130, 40; William Stanley, *The Faith and Practice of a Church of England Man* (London, 1688), pp. 144–63.

21. [Edward Lake], *Officium Eucharisticum*, 8th ed. (Dublin, 1683), pp. 98–103.

22. Jeremy Taylor, *The Rule and Exercises of Holy Living*, in *The Whole Works of the Right Reverend Jeremy Taylor*, eds. Reginald Heber and Charles Page Eden, 10 vols. (London, 1855–65), 3:101, 105–6, 16, 130–33, 190.

23. *Historical Manuscripts Commission Reports: Calendar of the Manuscripts of the Marquess of Ormonde, K.P.*, n.s. 7 (London, 1912):513–27. I owe this reference to Dr. Horwitz. David Green, *Sarah Duchess of Marlborough* (New York, 1967), pp. 147, 171n, 278n.

24. William Sherlock, *A Practical Discourse Concerning Death*, 2d ed. (London, 1690), was originally a course of sermons before an audience of lawyers; [Richard Allestree], *The Gentleman's Calling* (London, 1687).

"the very meanest of the People," who must have found parts of it unsympathetic.[25] Then, too, servants no doubt had access to books that were directed more obviously to their masters and mistresses.

It would probably be a mistake to equate the audience for this literature of religious direction with particular classes. The books were cheap enough and may have circulated sufficiently for almost anyone to have had access to them. Religious interest, rather than wealth, may have determined the audience for such a literature, as it may have set the bounds of literacy itself.

Another possible difficulty in equating production with popularity is that in areas far from London even families that could buy books may have had a limited choice. One bookseller in Chester who supplied others (probably schoolmasters in Cheshire, Lancashire, and Wales) with small lots of books, offered *A Week's Preparation towards a Worthy Receiving of the Lord's Supper* along with his ten textbook titles. It was bought most commonly in lots of twelve, and for any who may have depended on him for their religious reading the option was to take this or nothing.[26] On the other hand, a bookseller in as remote a spot as Hereford was offering seventy different religious books in his stock of 164 titles, according to an inventory of 1695.[27]

Finally, the seventeenth century saw the beginnings of lending libraries that may have extended the readership of these and other books.[28] Almost a hundred endowed libraries had been founded by 1700, and Thomas Bray had found another fifty parochial and lending libraries to assist with small grants. Most of these libraries were religious in inspiration and content, and might serve as parochial, school, and lending libraries, with varying degrees of accessibility to the public.[29] Bray also sent small libraries to mission districts and poor or remote parishes, mostly in Wales and America. But they were primarily for the use of ministers, in order that they might maintain the intellectual superiority that was coming to be expected

25. Rawlet, *Christian Monitor*, pp. 2, 39–53, 61.
26. H. R. Plomer, "A Chester Bookseller, 1667–1700," *The Library*, n.s. 4 (1903):373–83.
27. F. C. Morgan, "A Hereford Bookseller's Catalogue of 1695," *Woolhope Naturalists' Field Club Transactions, 1942–44*, pt. 1 (1945):22–36.
28. Alan Dugald McKillop, "English Circulating Libraries, 1725–1750," *The Library*, 4th ser. 14 (1934):477–85; Richmond P. Bond, "Early Lending Libraries," *The Library*, 5th ser. 13 (1958):204–5.
29. Kelly, *Early Public Libraries*, pp. 244–66, 50–96, 118, 143–44.

of them. There was some dissatisfaction at the inaccessibility of
these libraries to the general public.[30] Collections available in the
coffee houses do not appear to have included religious literature
of a noncontroversial sort, but inns sometimes had sermons and
similar matter for their guests.[31]

Even where library lists are available it is often impossible to
determine what popular works were included in public or private
collections. If they were catalogued at all, it was often too casually
("Sermons," "Meditations") to be identified. The library of Manchester Church, which was put together by several Presbyterian
clergymen in the 1650s, contained none of our titles. In fact it was
lacking any books smaller than quarto, which may mean that popular works were not catalogued or that they were considered easy
to come by otherwise. Perhaps the trustees felt that they could
perform the greatest service by making available quartos whose
average cost was around four shillings and folios averaging almost
twelve shillings.[32] Accounts of other parish and cathedral collections also indicate interests on a more scholarly plane.[33]

In short, the considerable degree of literacy, the cheapness of at
least some printed matter, the inns which gave these works a wider
audience, and the expectation that they would be read if given away
suggest a very wide readership. But there are reasons for thinking
that many Englishmen were not part of the religious culture represented by these or any other religious books. And this was not a
matter of class, any more than the audience for religious literature
was. There was, of course, the Restoration's famed smart set, more
embarrassed by its religion than by its vices, and maintaining the
traditional aristocratic ethic in which "pryde is but a pointe of gen-
trye; glouttonie, good fellowship; anger and revenge, but an effect

30. Edgar Legare Pennington, "The Reverend Thomas Bray," *The Church
Historical Society, Publications* 7 (Philadelphia, 1934):10–14; George Macau-
lay Trevelyan, *England Under Queen Anne*, 3 vols. (London, 1930–34), 1:48;
Mary Clement, *The S.P.C.K. and Wales, 1699–1740* (London, 1954), pp. 46–47.

31. George S. McCue, "Libraries of the London Coffee Houses," *Library
Quarterly* 4 (1934):624–27; J. Wickham Legg, *English Church Life From the
Restoration to the Tractarian Movement* (London, 1914), p. 5.

32. J. E. Bailey, "The Old 'English Library' of Manchester Church," *Notes
and Queries*, 5th ser. 8 (1877):61–63, 81–83.

33. R. P. Flindall, "Theological Reading in the Seventeenth Century,"
Church Quarterly Review 166 (1965):171–78; Paul Kaufman, "Reading Vogues
at English Cathedral Libraries of the Eighteenth Century," *Bulletin of the New
York Public Library* 67 (1963):643–72.

of courage; lecherye and wantonnes, a trycke of youth."[34] But there was also an underworld of the unchurched which was beginning to cause enough concern even to outweigh sectarian rancor.

Historians wonder how far the magical tradition of the medieval peasant had ever been included within Christianity. The strange intransigence of the early Puritans against what today seem trifling matters of ritual and church decoration is more understandable if these were still powerful symbols of an entirely alien cult. And it has been the persistence of magical traditions into the seventeenth century, and even beyond, that has occupied historians recently.[35]

Of course, the Scottish highlands were presumed to be outside the religious pale and possibly in the grip of witchcraft cults, until the lowlander missions of the eighteenth century.[36] The condition of Wales, with its soothsayers and bards, had likewise long troubled the Puritans. And the need to Christianize England itself was used as an argument for postponing missions to the American aborigines.[37] Conscientious ministers sent to outlying districts were horrified at the superstition and ignorance they encountered, as when an eighteenth-century Evangelical reported the worship of Barguest, the phantom dog of the moors, and other strange rites in the West Riding.[38] Some of the most surprising stories, as of the thirty communicants in Lincolnshire who could not say how many gods there were, and the man in Lancashire who could not remember having heard the name Jesus, concern not pagans but churchgoers, some of whom may never have heard a sermon or been served communion in their lives.[39] After the blows which were dealt to ecclesias-

34. Parsons, *A Christian Directorie*, p. 393.

35. See Keith Thomas, *Religion and the Decline of Magic* (New York, 1971), pp. 56, 71–72, 110, 145, 248, 453, 595, 608, 667, for nineteenth-century survivals.

36. Duncan Anderson, *The Bible in Seventeenth-Century Scottish Life and Literature* (London, 1936), p. 111, cf. p. 211; Trevelyan, *England Under Queen Anne*, 2:213, 218.

37. J. E. C. Hill, "Puritans and 'the Dark Corners of the Land,'" *Transactions of the Royal Historical Society*, 5th ser. 13 (1963):81, 96–97; see also Christopher Hill, "Propagating the Gospel," *Historical Essays 1660–1750; Presented to David Ogg*, ed. H. E. Bell and R. L. Ollard (London, 1963), pp. 35–59.

38. G. R. Balleine, *A History of the Evangelical Party in the Church of England* (London, 1909), p. 64.

39. Hill, "Puritans and 'the Dark Corners of the Land,'" pp. 98n1, 79–84; James Hitchcock, "Popular Religion in Elizabethan England" (Ph.D. diss., Princeton University, 1965), pp. 83–85; John Stoughton, *History of Religion in England*, 6 vols. (London, 1881), 5:231.

tical discipline in the Civil Wars, it became easier for England's old believers to find shelter in religious anonymity, and it was clear that after 1660 many were going to neither church nor chapel and differed little from the beggars who were generally assumed to be atheists.[40]

Churchmen often expressed their anxiety over this state of affairs in terms of how few were attending communion. The compulsory Easter communion was in some places attended by as few as ten per cent of the population.[41] Even when they went to church to avoid the fines, many refused to participate, "out of a rude clownishness."[42] Several reasons were given for this decline and others can be guessed. There was resentment over the expulsions of conscientious clergymen in 1604, the 1640s, 1662, and 1690, and the shortage of resident curates. Many used the excuse that they were not spiritually prepared for communion, and others that they had no suitable clothes and nothing to put in the collection.[43] Still others were protesting kneeling, or the character of the minister or of their fellow communicants. The last of our books to be written recorded a new candor in the objection of some, that "they have not found any benefit at all by it, and therefore they cannot conceive to what purpose they should give themselves the trouble of coming to it any more."[44]

Perhaps the reason these noncommunicants were not more noticeable by their absence was hinted by the same author, who mentioned that "In some Parishes the number of Communicants is so vastly great, that they cannot possibly communicate all at one time." In some places this crowding represented a rise in population, in others, the decay of England's medieval churches. Baxter wrote that even before the Fire three of London's suburban parishes contained sixty thousand inhabitants each, two others thirty thousand,

        40. Every, High Church Party, pp. xiii–xiv; C. W. Chalklin, Seventeenth-Century Kent (London, 1965), p. 224; Christopher Hill, Society and Puritanism in Pre-Revolutionary England (London, 1966), pp. 472–73. See Thomas, Religion and the Decline of Magic, pp. 159–73, for other evidence of ignorance, indifference, and unbelief.
        41. Chalklin, Kent, p. 224; Legg, English Church Life, p. 39; Norman Sykes, From Sheldon to Secker (Cambridge, 1959), p. 26; Laslett, World We Have Lost, pp. 71–73.
        42. Quoted in Chalklin, Kent, p. 224.
        43. Rawlet, Christian Monitor, pp. 44–52.
        44. Sir William Dawes, The Great Duty of Communicating Explain'd and Enforc'd (London, 1721), pp. 27–37.

and others twenty thousand.[45] The situation deteriorated when eighty-nine of London's ninety-seven churches were damaged or destroyed by the Fire.[46] Despite attempts at rebuilding, the Parliamentary commission that investigated the situation in 1711 reported that thirty-six churches (or the equivalent in seating) were serving a London population, excluding Dissenters, estimated at 411,500. The resulting average of over 11,000 souls was thought so unsatisfactory that Parliament accepted the need to build fifty new churches, to bring the average to 4,750. Only twelve of the projected churches were actually built.[47]

Nor was the pinch felt only in London. It was estimated in 1677 that Lancashire needed three times the thirty-seven parish churches it had, long before industrialization began to attract population to the north.[48] In 1709 Swift guessed that five-sixths of the inhabitants of many towns could not get inside their churches.[49] The Civil War had taken a toll of country churches, many having been fortified and some destroyed for military reasons.[50] Simply repairing the war damage was cause for congratulation, quite aside from providing new churches for a growing population. And the decay of church fabric went back at least to Elizabethan neglect.[51] If the doctrine of purgatory had been a major spur to church-building in medieval times, Englishmen were now finding other ways to employ their capital.

Even where there was space in churches, pew rentals might keep seats vacant. Vestry orders sometimes stipulated that no one was to

45. Richard Baxter, *Reliquiae Baxterianae* (London, 1696), pt. 2, p. 396; pt. 3, p. 165.

46. *Victoria History of London* (London, 1909), 1:339–42.

47. Andrew Browning, ed., *English Historical Documents, 1660–1714* (London, 1953), p. 427. Dissenters, estimated at 101,500, were served by eighty-eight chapels. E. S. deBeer, "Places of Worship in London About 1738," in *Studies in London History*, ed. A. E. J. Hollaender and William Kellaway (London, 1969), pp. 394–98, indicates that the number of Anglican churches was underestimated.

48. *Historical Manuscripts Commission: Report on the Manuscripts of the late Allan George Finch, Esq.* (London, 1922), 2:140.

49. Jonathan Swift, *The Works of Jonathan Swift, D.D.*, ed. Thomas Roscoe, 6 vols. (New York, n.d.), 5:248. Baxter, *Reliquiae*, pt. 2, p. 396, refers disapprovingly to 4,000 in some town and country parishes.

50. C. H. Firth, *Cromwell's Army*, 4th ed. (London, 1962), p. 166.

51. W. K. Jordan, *Philanthropy in England, 1480–1660* (London, 1959), pp. 298–320, and idem, *The Charities of London, 1480–1660* (London, 1960), pp. 298–307, 268.

sit above his "quality."[52] Furthermore, we cannot assume that people were crowding into the little space that was available; complaints of slack attendance go back before the Restoration.[53]

Now that the masses were drawn to communion not by any prospect of the Real Presence but by civic duty, their reluctance became discouragingly apparent. The designation "communicant" took on a new meaning when it was the only indication of Anglican adherence and churchmen promoted something of a eucharistic cult. Even before the Toleration Act, authors plaintively recommended that their readers communicate ostentatiously, as a kind of advertisement for the Church.[54] Banding together in voluntary religious societies, which began shortly after the Restoration, was an admission of the isolation felt by churchmen. These societies often ended in nothing more than a group devoted to daily communion, but some of them had envisioned living in semimonastic retirement.[55] And those which concentrated on missions and moral reform also seemed an acknowledgment that churchmen were now viewing English society from the outside.

Even so, while it is apparent that an indeterminate number of Englishmen existed at various removes from the culture represented by our books, there is evidence of widespread religious concern simply in the output of the religious press. If 95,000 copies was indeed the total of eighteen editions of Rawlet's work, by 1706, with apparently twenty-six editions, one household in ten in England and Wales might have owned a copy, by Gregory King's estimate of the population.[56] The Whole Duty of Man enjoyed the greatest number of editions between 1660 and 1711, perhaps forty-five in all, again probably enough copies (135,000) for every tenth family. And these works did not achieve this popularity only for lack of competition. For, although the forty-two best sellers studied

52. Esther deWaal, "New Churches in East London in the Eighteenth Century," Renaissance and Modern Studies 9 (1965):113.
53. Godfrey Davies, "Arminian vs. Puritan in England, ca. 1620–1640," Huntington Library Bulletin 5 (1934):176–77.
54. Stanley, Faith and Practice, pp. 68, 75, 98–100, 87.
55. Legg, English Church Life, pp. 281–302.
56. Browning, English Historical Documents, pp. 515–17. I have not tried to correct King's overestimate (see David V. Glass, "Gregory King's Estimate of the Population of England and Wales, 1695," Population Studies 3 [1950]: 338–74) since there were English readers in Scotland, Ireland, and America who should be added to his figures and Welsh who should be subtracted.

here may have accounted for somewhere between a third and a fifth of all copies of religious books produced in England in this period, there were another 250 titles with four editions or more, and over a thousand others which were sufficiently in demand to require at least the one reprinting that proved a lively interest. England had, of course, already accumulated large numbers of religious works before 1660, religious titles amounting to perhaps 44 per cent of all English editions until as late as 1640.[57] In the period 1660–1700, half of all works that required at least six editions were religious, as were two-thirds of those with twelve editions or more.[58] Not only is it obvious that religion was the major concern of the English reading public; it appears that in distribution these best sellers compare closely with best sellers in the twentieth century.[59] As with Bible production, this evidence suggests that the religious reading public stretched down into the half of England's population that King estimated to be economically dependent.

To be sure, one may wonder what might have sold best if the press had been free from government censorship. Certainly some kinds of literature would have seen greater sales had they not been produced and sold surreptitiously. But there is no reason to suppose that the standards of the reading public were so different from those that were officially maintained that heretical or salacious literature would have challenged the popularity of the books under consideration here. Free thought and immodesty had regularly been available in the form of the classics and translations of the classics, and yet the book trade was not sustained by baiting the censors.[60]

57. Edith L. Klotz, "A Subject Analysis of English Imprints for Every Tenth Year from 1480 to 1640," *Huntington Library Quarterly* 1 (1938):417–19. Since editions of religious books were probably larger than average editions the number of copies, as opposed to editions, for specifically religious works may be even greater than her figure of 44 per cent.

58. See my article, "On the Distribution of Religious and Occult Literature," p. 224n15, for a list of the nonreligious authors. These figures were based on Wing's *Short-Title Catalogue* alone; a search of the revised edition will probably inflate the figures but not change the proportions.

59. In the United States, the only books with an all-time sale reaching the 10 per cent of all families estimated for Allestree's and Rawlet's works (i.e., 5,500,000 copies) are two dictionaries, two cookbooks, an atlas, a poetry anthology, Spock's *Baby and Child Care*, Carnegie's *How to Win Friends and Influence People*, Kennedy's *Profiles in Courage*, along with perhaps two dozen undistinguished novels. Alice Payne Hackett, *70 Years of Best-Sellers, 1895–1965* (New York, 1967), pp. 11–13.

60. Lucretius did enjoy a vogue in the 1680s and 1690s, but his Latin editions were probably small.

In 1711, Convocation cited the restoration of licensing as the realm's most pressing spiritual need.[61] But these clerics certainly did not have the most popular literature in mind, which was nothing if not traditional and edifying. For the English reading public had shown itself more interested in religion than in any other subject.

A final problem concerning the reading public is the possibility of making a separation between Anglican and Dissenting audiences. The best sellers themselves occasionally recommended other books of their own persuasion, and they frequently took swipes at the opposed camp.[62] Few, if any, would have been welcomed equally by either party. But none of the books were polemics, and those by Dissenters must have appealed to some churchmen in order to achieve the kind of popularity required here. The number of actual nonconformists was probably not much more than 5 per cent of the population as shown by the religious survey of 1676.[63] Five per cent of King's estimate of families (i.e., 70,000) would fall short of the probable production of several of the Dissenters' works, whereas 40 per cent of the editions of these best sellers went to books by Dissenters. It may be that nonconformists were wealthier on the average, more interested in religious matters, and more dependent on books for their spiritual welfare than were Anglicans, and that they hoarded the books by Dissenting authors. But that would still leave many of their books for that group of Englishmen who for one reason or another conformed after 1660, but who were not entirely in sympathy with their parson or Church. In short, it is not unreasonable to speak of separate poles toward which the books—their themes and attitudes—might tend, even though we cannot speak of entirely distinct audiences.

---

61. [Canterbury Convocation], A *Representation of the Present State of Religion, With regard to the late Growth of Infidelity, Heresy and Profaneness*, corrected edition (London, 1711), pp. 4, 13, 20.

62. Allestree recommended Hammond's *Catechism*, and Hammond in turn wrote a preface for the *Whole Duty of Man*, as well as one for Richard Sherlock's work. Ken, Lake, Rawlet, Stanley, and Patrick also recommended the *Whole Duty*. "G. B." and Stanley mentioned numerous Anglican authors. Dissenters Russell, Mead, and Calamy recommended various Puritan writers.

63. Browning, *English Historical Documents*, pp. 413–16. Browning thought the census was "accurate enough" (p. 361), despite the wish of the bishops to minimize the number of nonconformists. S. A. Peyton, "The Religious Census of 1676," *English Historical Review* 48 (1933):99–104, and W. M. Wigfield, "Religious Statistics Concerning Recusants of the Stuart Period," *Theology* 41 (1940): 99–102, confirm some of the census figures by local studies.

Restoration England enjoys the reputation of an open and inquisitive society, from its irreverent aristocracy down to its heterodox poor. But despite poverty and illiteracy the output of England's cheap religious press was staggering. The total number of copies of just the works chosen for this study could easily have provided a book to every household in the realm, leaving out of account the thousands of other religious titles published in this period and the accumulation from earlier years. And since it seems that we can discount the effects of censorship, ideological philanthropy, and library circulation, these most popular books may reasonably be taken as the best evidence of the popular religious mind.

3. The Religious Best Sellers
of Restoration England

By 1660 the printing industry in England was nearly two centuries old, old enough for some books that had once enjoyed considerable popularity to have fallen out of favor. Arthur Dent's *The Plain Man's Path-Way to Heaven*, Thomas Sorocold's *Supplications of Saints*, Stephen Egerton's *Brief Method of Catechizing*, and *Eikon Basilike*, had all sold close to forty editions before that year, but were no longer in vogue. It is not always obvious why some of these declined in popularity, or why attractive works like Henry Scougal's *The Life of God in the Soul of Man* and John Austin's *Devotions in the Ancient Way of Offices* were not among those that replaced them in popularity. But it is often possible to identify some quality in the best sellers which might have accounted for the vagaries of fashion. And while we consider each of the most popular religious works with this purpose in mind, it will also be possible to indicate some of the themes and conflicts to be taken up in detail in later chapters.

Of particular interest are those works which maintained their popularity through the whole period. The oldest of our best sellers and the only one by a foreign author was *The Imitation of Christ* by Thomas à Kempis, often known to seventeenth-century readers as *The Following of Christ* or *The Christian's Pattern*. Its theme of the vanity of this world and contentment in God's will (categories J1, H8) was carried further than in the contemporary literature, and there is a spirit of timelessness in the book which contrasts with the urgency of seventeenth-century authors. No "Calvinist" writer

33

showed a greater longing to be resigned to God's overmastering will, and the patience which characterized the author's view of the spiritual life set this work off from those written in a later, more energetic age.

Not least among the changes in the two centuries between the composition of this book and that of any of the rest was the rise of printing, and the difference that made to the mentality of writers is apparent in several ways. The attack upon learning which begins and ends the *Imitation* is unparalleled in the later books, which were themselves evidence of the closer contact between lay readers and intellectuals and of a greater dependence upon the learned for moral and intellectual direction. The *Imitation*, unlike most of the later works, contains individual sentences and paragraphs that can stand alone, giving the book an aphoristic and "oral" character. In fact, some editions of the *Imitation* were printed in the form of aphorisms. And finally, no later author dared to put so much of his message into the mouth of God in the form of dialogues. For, after the Bible was widely printed and known at first hand, authors were more careful to quote Scripture in representing God's mind to their readers.

But despite an old-fashioned air there were many points of similarity with the later works. The passing references to purgatory, the mass, and intercessory saints could have been forgiven in an author who had lived so long before the Reformation, particularly in light of his slighting remarks on relics and pilgrimages. Even Dissenters might have been appeased by his rather ambiguous use of concepts which were translated into the familiar terms of "election" and "conversion" and by his insistence on grace as necessary in stimulating any good work.[1] And generally, in its theme of self-denial, in its suspicion of the motives and standards of its age, the *Imitation* was in character with other popular works, as it was in its distribution of interests as measured quantitatively. Of our later authors, the Puritan Lewis Bayly cited the book and the Anglican Jeremy Taylor often relied upon it, but it could not, of course, be associated with either party in the English church.

I have classified Lewis Bayly's *The Practice of Piety* with the works by Puritan and Dissenting authors despite the fact that Bayly was made Bishop of Bangor in 1616, shortly after the book first

1. Thomas à Kempis, *Of the Following of Christ*, trans. F. B. (n.p., 1624), pp. 37, 30, 53, 62, 77, 370.

appeared. He was, however, in constant trouble with his superiors even after his elevation, and is usually treated as a Puritan.[2] Whether or not Bayly himself is properly so characterized, his book proclaimed itself Puritan in its retort to those who call "*Zeale* in Religion, *Puritanisme*, . . . scruple of *conscience, Precisenesse.*"[3] Its absorption in sabbatarianism and the question of election makes it practically the stereotype of the Puritan manual, and it does more closely resemble Dissenting than Anglican books in its interests and attitudes, as measured quantitatively. A long and shapeless work, it opens with an erudite discussion of the nature of the Trinity and the names of God, then dilates on the misery of man from birth to death, on the happiness of the saints in life and death, on temptation and sin, on daily devotions, the fasts and feasts, sickness, death, and Christ's passion. It is not an inspiring or affecting work, but Bayly was clearly a man of considerable intelligence. And indeed his wit brings to mind the "metaphysical" poets of the day, especially in the concluding "Divine Colloquie between the Soule and her Saviour."

Another of the older Puritan books was Samuel Smith's *The Great Assize, or Day of Jubilee*, first published in 1615. It is a contentious, even vengeful work, whose constant theme is the near approach of judgment and the vindication of God's hard-pressed people. Smith clearly expected the state itself to be among his enemies, as well as Epicurean atheists who denied the Resurrection, and common worldlings who abused the godly. From abroad the Catholics threatened invasion and persecution, which Smith feared would lead to national apostasy.[4] There is no indication that he considered that these enemies could be recovered by God's mercy, and the book was certainly not written for this purpose but rather to encourage the elect. His feeling that the world was already irrevocably divided for judgment might have been the corollary of the views on election which he presented at some length. But further, unconscious commitment to it is indicated by his attraction to the story of Dives and Lazarus, to which he returns again and again in expression of his vindictiveness. The last section of the book is a separate sermon,

---

2. C. J. Stranks, *Anglican Devotion* (London, 1961), pp. 37–40, 62–63; H. R. Trevor-Roper, *Archbishop Laud, 1573–1645* (London, 1940), p. 188; Gordon S. Wakefield, *Puritan Devotion* (London, 1957), p. 4.
3. Bayly, *Practice of Piety*, p. 173.
4. *The Great Assize, or Day of Jubilee*, 8th impression (London, 1638), pp. 29–53, 156–58, 368–82.

A Fold for Christ's Sheepe, in which a discussion of Christ's love for the church is again turned into an attack on popery, atheism, and worldliness, and an exhortation to gird against persecution. One may assume that the work, which was reprinted well into the eighteenth century, appealed mostly to those who were facing the disabilities and ostracism of nonconformity. And Smith did have a graphic and vigorous style that makes that popularity understandable.

The last of the older works which maintained its popularity to the end of our period is *The Posie of Godlie Prayers*, by Nicolas Themylthorpe, Esquire, "one of the Quenes majesties sewers" or servers. The Queen indicated may have been James's consort, Anne of Denmark, since the book first appeared in 1608,[5] and the author was probably from the Norfolk family which sent a number of its sons to Oxford. The prayers are repetitious, the same few thoughts on repentance, amendment, dependence, and praise recurring with little variation. They do show a spirit of simplicity and serenity which gives the work some charm, but at the price of detachment from the affairs of life; the "gentle reader" to whom the book was addressed was expected to be in retirement from the world. As in the case of Thomas à Kempis, Themylthorpe could not be positively associated with either party in the Church, and his work could have appealed to them both.

Jeremy Taylor is still a familiar name in the history of English prose style, and two of his works were sufficiently popular among contemporaries to be considered here, *The Rule and Exercises of Holy Living* (first appearing in 1650) and *The Golden Grove; or a Manual of Daily Prayers and Litanies* (1655).[6] Both books were written under Puritan rule, and both were prefaced with bitter attacks on those who had despoiled the English Church and government, and on the "willingly seduced multitude."[7] There is nothing in the Dissenting literature which matched the intemperance of these attacks. And none of the other authors matched Taylor's refinement of intelligence and style.

Holy Living begins with an appeal against idleness, directed to

5. Nicolas Themylthorpe, *The Posie of Godlie Prayers* (Aberdeen, 1636). See Arber, *Registers*, 3:162, for date.
6. Another of Taylor's famous works, *Holy Dying*, had not achieved quite the popularity of its companion when they began to be bound together in editions after 1680, carrying the edition numbers proper for *Holy Living*.
7. *Holy Living*, p. 1.

the gentry who, Taylor felt, had failed England religiously and politically (pp. 3, 9–16). It continues with sections on devotion, sobriety, social justice (both "distributive"—the justice due to the different ranks in society—and "commutative," between equals), and ends with a discussion of religious duties and a section of prayers. Taylor is notable for the amount of space he devotes to affliction, work as a religious duty, the reverence due one's social superiors, and contentment in one's station (G8–9, H6–8). The work contains the only extended moral casuistry in the popular literature and is quite exceptional in its severity against sins of the flesh (G2). None of the others spent so much time condemning sensuality or advocated such specific mortifications of the body. The imagery for sin, too, is more sensual than legal, terming it pollution and sickness, and dwelling on man's "impurity" rather than on his alienation from God (pp. 53, 159, 195, 202–3). Virtue was likewise thought of in sensual terms. No other popular work advocated celibacy as a higher state than marriage, or introduced religiously erotic prayers for professed virgins. Indeed, Taylor expressed the fear that he was being so specific in these matters that the unclean might use his book for lewd purposes (pp. 55–65, 112).

Far from being a "Puritan" emphasis, the concentration on fleshly sins came, in Taylor's case, from Catholic sources and particularly from St. Francis de Sales.[8] As will be seen, the Dissenting tradition was more troubled by sins of the mind, and Taylor's emphasis is to be associated with his semi-Pelagian views of the nature of man and his desire to preserve a baptismal innocence. There are also frequent echoes of the *Imitation of Christ* in both of his best sellers, particularly in regard to giving up one's will to an earthly superior and to avoiding worldly affairs.

Taylor's *Golden Grove* originally appeared as a *Short Catechism for Children*, and was designed to ensure that the rising generation would not be left in entire ignorance of the principles of a disbanded Church.[9] Like all Anglican catechisms, it contained directions for belief (in a section on the Apostles' Creed), worship (in sections on the Lord's Prayer and the sacraments), and life (in a section on the Ten Commandments). To these Taylor added several

8. Stanley Morison, *English Prayer Books*, 3d ed. (Cambridge, 1949), p. 117; Stranks, *Anglican Devotion*, p. 85.
9. *The Golden Grove; or a Manual of Daily Prayers and Litanies*, in *The Whole Works of the Right Reverend Jeremy Taylor*, 7:591.

litanies, prayers, and hymns. Taylor's unique themes reappear, including prayers for a virgin leaving celibacy for matrimony, which did not conceal the author's regret at this exercise of God's "overruling providence," and a hymn expressing the doctrine that the Virgin Mary travailed without pain (pp. 647, 651). The association of holiness with self-denial and suffering is made explicit; subduing the flesh to the spirit and offering violence to one's appetites is represented as "an excellent abbreviation of the whole duty of a Christian" (pp. 619–20, 623). For this reason a major part of one's devotions was to be meditation on Christ's pain and shame. And there was again the emphasis on diligence in one's calling that we have learned to associate with the doctrine of God's election, coming from a writer who was out of sympathy with any Reformed understanding of that doctrine (pp. 611, 613–17, 597, 608).

The most popular religious work in Restoration England was *The Whole Duty of Man* (1657), which has been sufficiently proven to be the work of Richard Allestree.[10] Allestree contributed two other books to our list of early best sellers, making him the favorite author of his age. Writing during the Interregnum, he shared Taylor's fears for the survival of an Anglican piety, his moralistic understanding of Christianity, and to a large extent his literary skill.

Historians have sometimes assumed from the popularity of this work that it occupied a middle ground in the field of religious debate at the time, avoiding doctrinal controversy to deal in the common currency of moral teaching. But in fact the very title was provocative, coming as it did from the rather exceptional book of Ecclesiastes (12:13): "Fear God, and keep his commandments: for this is the whole duty of man." While Dissenters could have accepted this unevangelical statement with substantial qualifications, their fears would have been confirmed by the author's fondness for the equally exceptional epistle of James, with its legalistic emphasis. Allestree did not expend his ink in arguing these points but put down as simply as possible, "especially for the meanest reader," the whole of Christian religion under the organizing principle of man's duties, and not as a Dissenter might have done, in terms of God's plan. As a compendium of advice on moral conduct and social relations, the book would scarcely have been objectionable to any group except the more egalitarian Quakers. It was only in its guise

10. Paul Elmen, "Richard Allestree and *The Whole Duty of Man*," *The Library*, 5th ser. 6 (1951):19–27.

as a spiritual manual that it would have seemed dangerously incomplete to more evangelical readers. Even at that, it touched on most of our subject categories in its systematic and sensible way. Allestree thoughtfully organized the book into seventeen "Sundays" and suggested that reading through one's duty could thus be accomplished three times a year. Presumably it was to be read continually thereafter, assuming a status in the churchman's household like that of the homilies in his parish church.[11]

The Countess of Morton's Daily Exercise was another Anglican work written under Puritan rule, although it was not published until 1665, years after the Countess's death in 1654. She was Lady Anne Douglas, daughter of Sir Edward Villiers and hence English despite her Scottish title. As the wife of Robert, Earl of Morton, she had been entrusted with escorting the Princess Henrietta Anne to France in 1646.[12] The book was a short devotional exercise, with daily and occasional prayers and meditations which constantly echo the Prayer Book, the Creed, and the Psalms. Revealing a simple, unaffected, and dependent spirit, it is a pleasant enough work if somewhat cool. Its popularity was probably aided by its aristocratic associations and by the fact that it could have been acceptable to Dissenters as well as Anglicans.

A Week's Preparation Towards a Worthy Receiving of the Lords Supper (1678) was identified only as the work of a "G. B.", though a prefatory attack on Dissent reveals it as the work of an Anglican cleric. Beginning with an allusion to the same verse from which Allestree drew his title, it seems also to have been influenced by Taylor or perhaps by the same Catholic tradition, with such apparatus as "the seven spiritual works of mercy" and "the six corporal works of mercy." There is an engaging warmth in its prayers and directions which is uncommon in the Anglican literature. In fact, it is so full of tears of repentance and thankfulness and of sensual devotional imagery that in 1737 there appeared a *New Week's Preparation* which had been purged of emotional elements. In his foreword to that later work, the Duke of Devonshire called the old

---

11. John Wesley turned against the *Whole Duty* after his conversion: G. Thompson Blake, "The Whole Duty of Man," *London Quarterly and Holborn Review* 183 (1958):296. And the early Evangelical Henry Venn wrote a *Complete Duty of Man* to combat the tendencies noted.

12. *Corrections and Additions to the Dictionary of National Biography* (Boston, 1966), pp. 60–61. Lady Anne, Late Countess of Morton, *The Countess of Morton's Daily Exercise*, 17th ed. (London, 1696).

one "a disgrace and reproach to the dignity of a rational nature."
He thought that it used "a manner of address more suited for a
dissolute lover than for an acceptable worshipper of the all-pure
and all-knowing God," stimulated no doubt by the "wanton appetites and wishes of unmarried men and friars."[13] This seems a rather
heavy assault on such a slight, repetitive, and clumsy production,
but its infectious enthusiasm had made it one of the best-selling
works. Still, there may have been others even then who were un-
comfortable with its talk of suffering and languishing with love,
of "embracing a crucified Saviour" and of the "ravishing consolation"
of serving Christ, all juxtaposed with a horror at man's foul and
vile pollutions.[14]

Edmund Calamy's *The Godly Man's Ark, or City of Refuge in the
day of his Distress* (London, 1657) originated as sermons on the
death of Mrs. Elizabeth Moore, and was intended to help others
to establish their "evidences" or assurance of heaven when faced
with death. As the exposition proceeds, however, more and more
of the Puritan author's time is spent attacking false assurance. Presumption is associated in Calamy's mind with the sectarian and
atheistic errors which grew out of "Antimagistratical and Antimin-
isterial" doctrines. He laments the abandonment of the public worship and with it "that humble and exact walking with God in all
good duties, both towards God, and man, which was the credit, and
honour of the good old Puritan in former daies." To those who
exhibited this humility and strictness, Calamy was only too willing
to offer assurances, whereas to the rest God's only promise was "to
avenge his elect of all their enemies" (sigs. B5–B6ᵛ, p. 215). The last
twenty pages contain Mrs. Moore's own collection of "evidences,"
which tend to be of an emotional nature—feelings of loathing for
her "Leprosie of sin" and of exaltation that her soul has been "transplanted with Christ" (pp. 237–48).

Despite its title, Thomas Doolittle's *Treatise Concerning the
Lord's Supper* (1665) is also primarily on the subject of assurance
of salvation. And again, there is the same juxtaposition of "*a God of
infinite jealousie*" who threatens to aggravate the damnation of unworthy worshippers, with some of the most glowing affective mysti-

13. S. C. Carpenter, *Eighteenth Century Church and People* (London,
1959), p. 192.
14. [G. B.], *A Weeks Preparation Towards a Worthy Receiving of the Lords
Supper* (London, 1679), pp. 76, 62, 11, 18, 26, 51.

cism in the literature.[15] His artlessness is too apparent in his assertion of the gratuitous character of God's love, which he proves by
the fact that God could have glorified Himself equally in man's
damnation, and that "if thou shalt be saved, there is no addition
made thereby to Gods happiness" (p. 73). Nowhere in the popular
literature is there a more horrific statement than Doolittle's com-
ment that an unworthy communicant is in effect "an Abettor and
Consenter" to Christ's death and that at judgment His blood will
"*cry against* you, instead of *pleading for* you" (pp. 42–43).[16] Yet
some twenty-three editions of this Dissenter's work were demanded
at a time when more pleasant books were passed over. First impressions may be misleading; a quantitative analysis shows the book to
be one of the highest on a scale of confidence as against anxiety,
and second among all books in attention to the happiness of the
godly (D6). The impression remains, nevertheless, of an intellectually tedious and emotionally exhausting work.

It is easier to account for the popularity of *The Great Concern:
or, A Serious Warning to a Timely and Thorough Preparation for
Death* by the Dissenter Edward Pearse. It first appeared in 1671,
shortly before the author's own early death, and is a surprisingly
cheerful work despite its theme. Pearse was not playing upon exaggerated fears. Death and persecution were facts of the seventeenth-
century Dissenters' lives, and Pearse's problem was how to meet
them with confidence in God rather than with bitterness. He does
not seem to think that the sufferings of the saints served principally
to fuel God's wrath, but expresses the hope that they may in some
way have furthered God's Gospel and the compassion of His people
for others.[17]

Joseph Alleine's *An Alarm to Unconverted Sinners* (1672) also
went under the titles *A Sure Guide to Heaven* and *Solemn Warn-
ings of the Dead*, and was one of several Dissenting works with an
evangelical purpose. It is a dramatic work with a gamey flavor of
what then passed for "the Language of Canaan," with its Biblical
conceits and frequent exclamations. His rendering of Isaiah 64:6
made "our Righteousness but a menstruous cloth," and he was so

15. Thomas Doolittle, *A Treatise Concerning the Lords Supper*, 20th ed.
(Boston, 1708), pp. 40–49.
16. He was expanding on 1 Cor. 11:27–29.
17. Pearse, *The Great Concern*, pp. 114, 125–27, 181.

taken with the expression that he later repeated it.[18] But he denied "playing the Orator to make a learned speech to you," or "dressing my dish with Eloquence, wherewith to please you." He was not "fishing for your applause, but for your souls," and for that, he said, "I would write unto them in tears, I would weep out every Argument, I would empty my Veins for Ink" (pp. 1–4). As with other Calvinists, one of his major difficulties concerned the objection of the immutability of God's election. Alleine's answer was that "Thou beginnest at the wrong end, if thou disputest first about thine Election. Prove thy Conversion, and then never doubt of thine Election." While it may be true that nothing can be done toward salvation without the Spirit of God, the Spirit draws near to those who wait expectantly (pp. 20, 114, 9). Alleine did feel it necessary to discriminate between his position and that of "Arminians," but a conditional tone in his own explanation of the calling is unmistakable. Most of the book is spent, not in defining conversion, but in belaboring the complacency and self-deception of his readers.

The Pilgrim's Progress from This World to That Which is to Come (1678) is still being published, the only one of our books to have established itself as a literary and religious classic.[19] This is astonishing not only in that John Bunyan had the least schooling of any of our authors, but also for the fact that he wrote under the greatest adversity. It was the only book written with humor, as distinguished from wit. There is pathos in the realization that his allegorical figures represented social as much as moral forces and that Bunyan transcended his circumstances by transforming his neighbors into the vices and virtues he found within himself. It is hardly to be supposed that all of his Dissenting readers could resist the temptation to change these figures back into their social enemies. But Bunyan's intention was evangelistic: the progress of the soul through conversion, temptation, adversity, assurance, testimony, and death. Despite a crabbed syntax and certain archaisms not found in the more literary English of the other writers, the work did resemble theirs, and nowhere more than in the exhortations which the pilgrims organized under the numbered points so dear to the preachers of the day.

18. Joseph Alleine, *An Alarm to Unconverted Sinners* (Boston, 1727), pp. 35, 127.

19. John Bunyan, *The Pilgrim's Progress from This World to That Which is to Come* (New York, 1964).

The remaining perennial best sellers are all by churchmen. Edward Lake's *Officium Eucharisticum. A Preparatory Service to a Devout and Worthy Reception of the Lords Supper* (1673) was written for the courtly world and dedicated to the future Queen Mary, whose chaplain Lake was. But the tone and the directions given differed little from those that Allestree had directed to the poor, and indeed Lake recommended the *Whole Duty of Man*. The term "Anglican" is entirely appropriate to the work, for Lake professed to have been inspired by the "Devout Fathers" of the Church of England, Andrewes, Cosin, and "that Great and Good Man, Archbishop Laud."[20] He may also have been indebted to Taylor, in his care over an exact confession, his belief in *"acting revenge upon thy self by Fasting*, and other acts of *Mortification,"* and his clearly conditional understanding of justification (pp. 117, 146–59). And, as in Taylor's case, it is unsettling to find the clearest connection between grace and riches in this book, which is also the most clearly anti-Calvinist. There is no question of concealed sympathy with a Puritan mentality; Lake makes a point of his indifference as to how the book is received by those "whose unwieldly Zeal has transported them under a pretence of spuing out Popery" (sig. A4ᵛ, pp. 6, 129).

Thomas Ken's *A Manual of Prayers for the Use of the Scholars of Winchester College* (London, 1675) was in the same semi-Pelagian tradition, as shown in its hope of capturing the minds of boys before they were polluted, so that "your duty will grow natural to you." He did not challenge the universally accepted view that " 'tis God that works in you to will and to do of his good pleasure," but he was more concerned to remind readers that "God also commands you, to work out your own salvation your self" (pp. 2, 61), quoting the paradox from Philippians 2:12–13. To this end, Ken offered full directions for private devotions and confession. Like other Anglicans, he was not too bashful to allude to the "unclean thoughts" which will occur to schoolboys at night and to suggest confession of them in morning prayers. But he saw a danger in making boys overly scrupulous. He advised them, for example, not to worry about an inability to shed tears in confession, for "though tears are very desireable, yet they are not always signs of true Repentance" (pp. 17, 9, 5, 14, 23, 63–64).

Simon Patrick's *A Book for Beginners: or, An Help to Young*

20. *Officium Eucharisticum*, sig. A4.

Communicants (1679)[21] is the most interesting of those written with a younger audience in mind. The usual directions and prayers for communion appear, but there is also firm but friendly advice on the temptations of youth. We shall have more to say on his advice regarding the difficult position of children in an authoritarian society. Like Ken, Patrick was motivated to write by a belief in childish innocence, a desire to capture his young readers before they were "tainted and corrupted by vice and wickedness," and a desire to help them "glorify God with body and soul . . . in [their] best days." He also hoped to combat a waning respect for the clergy and Church among young people.[22]

The Excellence and Usefulness of the Common-Prayer was a printed sermon preached in 1681 by William Beveridge at the reopening of St. Peter's, Cornhill, fifteen years after it was damaged in the Great Fire. He used the occasion to justify the Church's forms of worship by a number of arguments that seem directed at disaffected Anglicans. There was no other way, he suggested, that the nation could be sure that all its churches' services were edifying and no better way to draw communities together than by common prayers. There was no better teaching method than liturgical repetition, which reaches the affections as well as the brain and insures against misunderstandings. Even chancel screens were defended against a fashionable plainness. They must have served some good purpose to have been in use for fourteen centuries, though what the reasons were "it is not necessary for us to inquire now." But the best argument for the Anglican mean in worship was the spiteful opposition of Papists on one hand and Puritans on the other.[23] Even those who may not have found his arguments compelling must have admired his relaxed and limpid style.

A second group of books, the earlier best sellers whose popularity declined toward the middle of our period, contains the last of the works composed before the Civil War. John Ball's *A Short Treatise Contayning all the Principall Grounds of Christian Religion*, some-

21. *DNB* gives the date as 1662 but appears to be in error. See Patrick, *A Book for Beginners*, 1: "To the Reader."
22. Ibid., "To the Reader," pp. 630, 621.
23. William Beveridge, *The Excellency and Usefulness of the Common-Prayer*, in *The Works of the Right Reverend Father in God, Dr. William Beveridge*, 2 vols. (London, 1720), 2:559–61.

times entitled *A Short Catechism*, cannot be traced back further than its seventh edition in 1629. A Puritan work, it was not meant for children and is not really so much a catechism as a topical index to the Bible, each of whose 226 sections contains a multitude of citations. It is the nearest thing to a theological text and presents the most metaphysical image of God among these popular works. Ball could be erudite in his answers, borrowing occasionally from the scholastics, but he was also one of the most gratifyingly succinct of the authors. All in all, the work gives a pleasant picture of a non-controversial Puritan divine, even though he routinely rejected several Catholic doctrines.[24]

The most mysterious of our authors was a John Hart, D.D., who published a number of chapbook-like tracts, some under the pseudonyms Andrew Jones and William Jones. His first pamphlets appeared in the late 1640s and six later ones achieved a marked popularity: *The Plain Man's Plain path-way to Heaven* (1656), *Christ's First Sermon* (1656), *Christ's Last Sermon* (?), *Black Book of Conscience* (1656), *Morbus Satanicus. The Devil's Disease: Or, The Sin of Pride arraigned and Condemned* (1662, tenth edition), and *Doomsday: or, The Great Day of the Lord drawing nigh* (1660). Hart seems a stranger to English educational or ecclesiastical records and may have been a Scot, perhaps the John Hart who served churches in Hamilton and then in County Donegal until ejected in 1662.[25] But there are no Scotticisms in his style and in three of the tracts he refers to his society as England. His attitudes and emphases are much closer to those found in the Dissenters' works, but because of uncertainty as to his affiliation the tracts have not been included with that group.

Hart's tracts could have been acceptable to readers of either party, not because they rose above the issues dividing Englishmen but because they hardly reached so high. Some of them appeared in the old black letter or gothic type, with woodcuts of death as a skeleton threatening a well-dressed family, or of courtesans with large beauty patches in the shape of stars, crescents, or crosses, and with the careless décolletage that disturbed Hart. He also reported

24. Ball, *Short Treatise*, pp. 135–37, 143, 149, 184, 208.
25. Hew Scott, *Fasti Ecclesiae Scoticanae*, 9 vols. (Edinburgh, 1915–61), 3:262. Jones is clearly the pseudonym, since the titles which are associated with that name never attempt other disguises such as Hart's J.H., I.H., Hart On-hi, or complete anonymity.

two prodigies that the other authors would have considered be-
neath their notice: a monster born in Spain with seven heads and
a satyr's body, and an Antwerp merchant's vain daughter whom
God gave over to the Devil and who, after a miserable death, existed as a loathsome and deformed black cat.[26] But the distance
between these tracts and the rest of the literature is not great in
subject or tone. Hart uses the familiar homiletical style and shows
the usual anxieties of the clerical elite. His constant themes are the
growth of blasphemy, atheism, and libertinism (extending even to
imposters claiming to be the Virgin Mary or Christ himself), the
imminence of God's judgment as the cup of England's wickedness
ran over, and the need to escape wrath by individual and national
repentance. Hart had not lost hope for the unregenerate, and, while
he admits man's powerlessness to repent and believe without the
Spirit's aid, he rejects as the Devil's invention a fatalistic or antinomian understanding of predestination.[27] There is, however, a
good deal of resentment shown toward gallants and haughty women
who, as in Isaiah's day, "walk with stretched out necks, and wanton
eyes; walking and mincing as they go, and making a tinkling with
their feet."[28] Pride, "the devil's disease," he associates with "naked
breasts" and painted faces, but also with social oppression. Riches
were certainly no token of God's favor, and Hart accepts as a commonplace the association of poverty with blessedness and riches
with judgment.[29] He freely admits that the wicked have more comfort and pleasure in this world, but then he does not suppose that
there is any other motive in religious duties than that of securing
heaven.

In short, the same themes that occupied the other authors appeared in Hart's tracts in slightly exaggerated forms. But they are
not treated so differently as to suggest a different audience. Taken

26. "Andrew Jones," *Dooms-day: or, The Great Day of the Lord drawing
nigh*, 25th ed. (London, 1678), sig. A5ᵛ; "Andrew Jones," *Morbus Satanicus.
The Devils Disease Or, The Sin of Pride arraigned and condemned*, 16th ed.
(London, 1667), sigs. B1ᵛ–B2ᵛ.
27. *Christs First Sermon*, 11th ed. (London, 1663), sigs. A5ᵛ–C2ᵛ; *Dooms-
day*, sig. A4ᵛ.
28. *Morbus Satanicus*, sigs. A2–A3ᵛ. Taylor quoted this verse (Isa. 3:16) to
the same purpose in *Holy Living*, p. 83.
29. *The Plain Mans Plain path-way to Heaven*, 53d ed. (London, 1675),
sigs. B2ᵛ–B3ᵛ; *Christ's Last Sermon* (London, 1679), sigs. B2, C4ᵛ, C8; *Dooms-
day*, sig. A7ᵛ; "Andrew Jones," *Black Book of Conscience*, 26th ed. (Boston,
1732), pp. 16–21.

together his pamphlets rank first in attention to Satan (category B12) and second in categories expressive of the sterner side of God's character. They are also first in emphasis on the threat of atheism (I19), on judgment and the afterlife (J3–7), and in categories revealing anxiety.[30] And yet they are often cheerfully colloquial despite these themes, and their very awkwardness of expression must have helped keep them from seeming as frightening as they ought to have been.

Thomas Brookes appears to have been something of an embarrassment to the Dissenting cause. In later years Edmund Calamy III wrote of him that "Though he used many homely phrases and sometimes too familiar resemblances, which to nice critics might appear ridiculous, he did more good to souls than many who deliver the most exact composures. And let the wits of the age pass what censures they please, 'He that winneth Souls is wise.' "[31] The book that would have been most familiar to the wits of the age was his *Apples of Gold for Young Men and Women: and A Crown of Glory for Old Men and Women* (1657), written to encourage the young to "be good betimes." Brookes did not add yet another analysis of conversion to the pile of books on that subject, but rather offered a flood of illustrations, metaphors, and allusions, from classical history, mythology, nature, and the Bible, to urge his readers to "seek the Lord." Some of these illustrations are less apt than others but they are interesting in their own right and give the book a buoyancy which the others lacked.

Richard Baxter took a different approach to writing on conversion in *A Call to the Unconverted* (1657). He gave credit for the idea behind his book to Archbishop Ussher, who had urged him to use "vehement persuasions" as "meeter than directions only."[32] Baxter was equal to the task, demonstrating an uncommon facility in expanding into a book the single theme of avoiding God's wrath. There is no lack of pungent expression: "sin is the brat of your own concupiscence, and not to be fathered on God." Men are so ready to take the Devil's suggestions that you "tempt him to tempt you. And it is easy to catch such greedy fish that are ranging for a bait, and will take the bare hook." His use of terror is entirely calculated:

30. For the typologies concerning God's character and anxiety, see chapters 5 and 6 below.
31. *The Non-Conformist's Memorial*, ed. Samuel Palmer, 2d ed., 3 vols. (London, 1802–3), 1:150.
32. Baxter, *Reliquiae*, pt. 1, p. 115.

"we would not so much as affright or trouble you with the name of damnation without necessity."[33] At other times he lures his readers to holiness by descriptions of the beauty and worth of a holy life. And, if he sometimes seems inspired by resentment against those who mock God's ministers, he does not despair of the conversion of any, "even to the drunkards, swearers, worldlings, thieves, yea, to the despisers and reproachers of the holy way of salvation" (pp. 503–5, 516).

Like others of the evangelistic authors, Baxter spent a good deal of time answering the objections of antinomians. It had become common of late, among the ungodly who were seeking an excuse, to argue that "We can do nothing without God; . . . if he have not predestinated us, and will not turn us, how can we turn ourselves or be saved?" Even Calvin, Baxter said, believed in free will (albeit a free will "disposed to evil"). This still left room for one to show a willingness to be changed: "Can you truly say, that you do as much as you are able to do? . . . If you will not do what you can, it is just with God to deny you that grace by which you might do more" (pp. 506–7). Baxter's subtlety did not stop there. "God hath two degrees of mercy to show: the mercy of conversion first, and the mercy of salvation last. The latter he will give to none but those that will and run, and hath promised it to them only. The former is to make them willing that were unwilling; and though your willingness and endeavours deserve not his grace, yet your wilful refusal deserveth that it should be denied unto you" (p. 533). An unwary reader was led to suppose that the question had always turned on whether man's willingness and endeavours deserved salvation, and not on whether willingness itself was in man's power. Having implicitly denied the irresistibility of grace, he went on to deny that Christ's atonement was limited to the elect. It was becoming impossible to assert, with the implacable logic of the Reformers, that God took pleasure in the damnation of the reprobate, and Baxter was ready to dispute with any who claimed as much (pp. 517–19). One senses his exasperation as he dismisses the subject: "The dispute about free-will is beyond your capacity." There were more important questions to be attended to, the ultimate one being "What is your resolution? Will you turn, or will you not?" (pp. 533, 521).

33. Baxter, *Call to the Unconverted*, pp. 534, 516.

Only three Anglican works were among the best sellers of the early period, all of them written under Puritan rule. Richard Sherlock's *The Principles of Holy Christian Religion* (1656) was an expansion of the Church Catechism which roughly triples its number of questions and responses. The people of England had been made "fickle and giddy" by an abundance of preaching without solid doctrinal training, and the late proliferation of catechisms had done as much harm as good at a time when the need was for a common "form of sound words."[34] So Sherlock set out to answer objections to Anglican liturgy and practice, including such maligned institutions as sponsoring by godparents, which creates "*Spiritual Kindred* among Christian Neighbours." He viewed regeneration in baptismal terms, with repentance and faith presented simply as acts of obedience to the baptismal vows (pp. 59–63, 25–28, 14).

For a book written expressly for the gentry to have sold perhaps fifty thousand copies meant that it reached a larger audience than intended. Richard Allestree's *The Gentleman's Calling* (1659) was not a general work, however, and takes us into a more stylish world than that of the other books. It was meant to break down the barrier between an aristocratic mentality and the Protestant ethos. The paradox of the title announced this intention. Allestree admitted that it was a commonplace that the essence of gentility was in having no specific calling, but he hoped to impress upon that class their responsibility to society and to religion.[35] He amused them: "Must *Gentlemen* buy Damnation, as they usually do Wares, dearer than other men?" He flattered and cajoled them: "Christian Life . . . will constantly provide you with innocent divertisements, nay much more, it will give you business, so excellent, and worthy the dignity of your Nature, so Noble and answerable to the Splendor of your Qualities, so every way agreeable to the aims of Rational Men . . . [and] so far from imploying any thing of real toil or uneasiness, that it is only an Art of refining and sublimating your Pleasures." He winked at those pleasures, submitting that since "gentlemen" are connoisseurs of "transitory Beauties" they should also be the best judges of the "more ravishing appearance" of virtue (p. 148, sigs. a3^v–a4, a^v). He appealed to their sense of duty, expanding on their advantages of education, wealth, time, authority, and reputa-

34. Richard Sherlock, *The Principles of Holy Christian Religion*, 12th ed. (London, 1676), sigs. A3–A5, quoting 2 Tim. 1:13.
35. Allestree, *Gentleman's Calling*, sig A4^v.

tion. And he frankly criticized them for their callous treatment of the poor, for their pose of atheism, and for their idle and ignorant worthlessness at a time of national humiliation (pp. 12–17, 73–74, 31–38, 128–31). Allestree's bitterest words were saved for a long attack on duelling, which showed up the contradictions of their way of life. How could a class which devoted itself to sensuality here seek suffering and martyrdom? And how could those who insisted on the world's respect kill each other like gladiators for the entertainment of their inferiors? "Who would not think *Bedlam* the only Seminary to breed Men up for such a Trade?" Why were those who gloried in their courage too afraid of public opinion to turn down these ridiculous challenges? And why did those who would not be governed by any rules create for themselves punctillios in this case? (pp. 135–47). Perhaps it was Allestree's mixture of envy and resentment of this class that struck a responsive chord in the general public.

Allestree's *The Causes of the Decay of Christian Piety* was also written under Puritan rule, though not published until 1667. It was in the witty style of *The Gentleman's Calling,* and expressed the same hope that the natural leaders of English society would dedicate themselves to bringing piety back into fashion.[36] There is no analysis of the causes of religious decline because, for Allestree, it could be traced ultimately to an inexplicable human perversity. But he divides his time between the various expressions of this decline—indifference, theological ignorance, sensuality, halfheartedness, disputes, pride, excessive curiosity, self-interest, and misplaced zeal. Sometimes it is the Puritans who are blamed for the decline, with their overemphasis upon God's mercy, their easy assurance and casuist conscience, and their destruction of the Church's discipline through schism (pp. 52–59, 155, 170–72). But at other times England's previous failings are thought to explain why God had allowed the scourge of Puritan rebellion, despite His signal care for the nation throughout history (pp. 190–92). It was presumably the further blows of plague and fire that induced Allestree to publish the manuscript.

The most gripping of all the books is a short firsthand account of these two catastrophes, in Thomas Vincent's *God's Terrible Voice in the City of London* (1667). It became a religious book in its

36. [Richard Allestree], *The Causes of the Decay of Christian Piety* (London, 1704), p. 35.

providential interpretation of the events, from God's earliest warning in Holland's plague of 1664, "not to speak any thing whether there was any signification and influence in the *Blazing-Star* not long before."[37] England's specific failures are not made more specific than charges of licentiousness and scoffing which would have been appropriate at any time, but there is an insinuation that it was the plight of the Dissenters that brought divine judgment. For it was the cowardice of the "ruffling Gallants," "spotted Ladies," and their guilty-minded conforming ministers in fleeing the plague that allowed the ejected ministers to play a heroic role in the story, tending the dying and preaching to unprecedented crowds (pp. 5, 15–18). The Dissenter's ill-concealed satisfaction at England's terror is made more chilling as his picture of London under the Plague merges with his image of Hell, and the Fire runs together with the destruction of Sodom, the desolation of Jerusalem, and the prophecies of the Last Days (pp. 10, 25–30). Vincent was out of sympathy with his own society to the extent that it did not occur to him to mention the Devil in connection with its misfortunes, although he did find a villain's role for Catholics who he believed had set the fire. But just as it was God who began to remit the plague after the public fast held by the remaining ministers, so it was God who directed the wind which spread that fire through a licentious city (pp. 18, 22–23).

The last of the books with an early popularity was Matthew Mead's *The Almost Christian Discovered* (1662). Its very existence, let alone its popularity, calls into question the view that Dissenters were motivated largely by the desire to smooth their anxieties, whether theological or social. For here is a beloved book whose purpose was to raise questions about the reader's spiritual state rather than to settle them. Twenty different assurances that had lured men asleep were demolished in turn, and their supposed scriptural justifications were met and overthrown by superfine distinctions. In the end, however, it does appear that it was only overconfidence which drew the cantankerous Mr. Mead out upon his congenial mission, for after grinding the last bits of self-confidence he was willing enough to offer hope to the truly humble.

---

37. [Thomas Vincent], *Gods Terrible Voice in the City of London* (Cambridge, Mass., 1668), p. 4.

Only one of the most popular religious works of the period 1689 to 1711 was by a Dissenter, Robert Russell's *Seven Sermons* (1697). The only remarkable feature of the book is the initial sermon, on the unpardonable sin, which was meant to assure readers of the unlikelihood of their having committed it. He understood the notion to mean an act of pure malice, in full awareness of the doctrine of God's love, as persecution of the Gospel would be.[38] The other sermons are on the familiar themes of prayer, conversion, death, and heaven, and are marked by a less emotional manner than the earlier Dissenters' works. But there is an undercurrent of the bitterness which separated Englishmen even after the Toleration. Though his Calvinist soteriology was tempered by a belief in an unlimited atonement, he was so familiar with the excuses that men put forward when approached with the Gospel that he had little hope for England even as a mission field (pp. 114, 124–34, 8, 179–81). Among "the best of People" there were many who neglected family prayers, at a time when Russell thought that the only hope for national "Reformation" rested at the level of "Houses and Families," that is, with the next generation (pp. 28–29, 193).

Not included with either party was William Penn's *A Key, Opening the Way to every Capacity; How to distinguish the Religion Professed by the People Called Quakers, from the Perversions and Misrepresentations of their Adversaries* (1692). This was a conciliatory tract, showing the extent of the Quakers' orthodoxy. Penn accepted some concept of the Trinity though without the "Schoolmen's" elaborations, he believed in the Resurrection without curiosity as to its mode, and he respected the Bible as witnessing to the true "Word of God" (i.e., Christ) while warning of the deadening effect of literalism.[39] But he was inviting violent objection by arguing that the sacraments were only for the infancy of the church, and by insisting on the other hand that corporate worship must follow the church's "Primitive Practice." The "Light Within" is explained as neither a natural endowment nor equivalent with the mystical in-

38. Robert Russell, *Seven Sermons*, 4th ed. (Boston, 1701), pp. 11–19, 123–26. Russell was identified as a minister at Wadhurst, Sussex, and was perhaps from the family of Russells that was associated with Oxford and that had supplied numerous clergymen to Sussex and Dorset.
39. William Penn, *A Key, opening the Way to every Capacity; How to distinguish the Religion Professed by the People Called Quakers, from the Perversions and Misrepresentations of their Adversaries*, in *A Collection of the Works of William Penn*, 2 vols. (London, 1726), 2:782–84, 787.

dwelling of God, but rather as a gift from God (pp. 784–85, 778–80). Penn was most eager to rebut the accusation of lawlessness or antinomianism and indeed to turn it back on the Quakers' critics. For it was the entire trust in God's grace or in one's beliefs which was responsible for the self-righteous indifference of many. Quakers, by contrast, saw salvation in a life of obedience, for "The very *Believing* is an Act of the Mind, *concurring* with God's working in or upon the Mind, and therefore a *godly work.*" It was therefore obvious why Quakers had proven the most law-abiding of men, honoring all men sincerely and without the world's way of flattery, showing respect for superiors in their obedience to all just laws, and giving the world a model of government in their local and regional administration (pp. 781–89). As an apology the work must have been successful to have required twelve editions in so short a time. But in the end, differences were minimized to the point that probably few were willing to make the rather slight adjustments of doctrine and behavior that seemed to be necessary, when making those adjustments meant sharing the Quakers' sufferings.

Of all the books, the one written with the most obvious intention of becoming a best seller was John Rawlet's *The Christian Monitor* (1686). It was purposely short, Rawlet said, so that it could be "more generally dispersed, and that amongst the very meanest of the People, and may more easily be read and remembered by such as have neither Time to read large Books, nor Money to buy them."[40] One can only wonder whether poor churchmen found his good intentions merely insulting, as when he informed them that the souls of the poor were as precious as those of the rich. The sins that engaged his attention were those of the flesh, perhaps as those more characteristic of the poor, and hell brought to mind not the Pharisee or the extortioner but drunkards and harlots (pp. 44–45, 49–55, 29). Rawlet, prevented by poverty from taking his B.A., was insistent on the duty of contentment: "I have been a little the larger upon this for the sake of poor People, who are apt to be discontent, and to murmer at their Condition; tho' alas, they commonly bring themselves into it, or make it much worse by their own careless and loose Lives." The poor must remember that their "low Condition

40. Rawlet, *Christian Monitor*, p. 2. Thomas Bray wrote *A Brief Account of the Life of the Reverend Mr. John Rawlet* (London, 1728), giving him credit for having inspired his own efforts to provide books and libraries for England (sigs. C1v–C4).

frees [them] from a great many Snares and Temptations, and from a great many Cares and Sorrows that rich People meet with." Even if they should starve "(which not one of a Thousand does in Times of Peace and Plenty)" yet heaven is promised to the dutiful. But it was not likely to come to that, for the respectable poor could usually count on the charity of their wealthier neighbors (pp. 39, 20–21). Again, these attitudes need not be associated with Calvinism when we find them in a work which most resembled the *Whole Duty of Man* in making obedience rather than conversion the essence of religion.

Perhaps the most surprising of the books is Dean William Sherlock's *A Practical Discourse Concerning Death* (1689), originally sermons designed for the lawyers of the Temple. Sherlock attempts a new evangelistic technique based on the latest psychological formulations. It comes as a shock to realize that he means hedonism, and that he means to use it rather than to refute it. On the assumption that men are naturally and properly motivated toward pleasure, it is up to the Christian apologist to demonstrate the superiority of the religious life in those very terms. And, in such a sensual age as his, Sherlock thought it was particularly the fear of death that dominated men's minds and was therefore the proper point of contact for the evangelist. He took for granted belief in an afterlife as "the belief of all mankind," so that "There is not a more effectual way to Revive the True Spirit of Christianity in the World, than seriously to meditate on what we commonly call the four last Things; Death, Judgment, Heaven, and Hell." He proceeds to argue that pleasure varies "proportionally to the length and certainty of its continuance" and to its suitability to our natures, and that on these counts the pleasures of religion are superior to those of the flesh. Indeed, hell itself may be no more than eternal desires for sensual gratifications which can not be fulfilled after death.[41] It is further shown that the doctrine of the afterlife helped the believer to live by faith, by weaning him from attachment to this world. The expectation of death at any moment would help one to resist fleshly temptations (pp. 70–76, 90–115), a doctrine that was given scope by the charnel poets of the next century. Sherlock can hardly be called morbid, despite his theme, but seems an urbane writer who had found that sustained argument was necessary to the Christian apologist in the new conditions of English culture.

41. William Sherlock, *Practical Discourse*, pp. 1–10.

Another of Bishop Beveridge's sermons, *Of the Happiness of the Saints in Heaven* (1690), was included in this group and shared Sherlock's evangelistic concern. It was never easy for an author to dwell on heaven's delights, because of the lack of tension in the theme, but Beveridge could contrast with them the disappointment that a sinner would feel in heaven, unable to see its light, hear its music, taste its sweetness, or participate in its joy. Of course his main purpose was to exhort his hearers to "apply" to Christ, who is always ready to assist man's efforts toward repentance and faith. Perhaps his readers needed this encouragement after reading his impossible description of the typical saint, as one abounding in good works, unaffected by temptation, and unmixed in his love for God.[42]

William Stanley's *The Faith and Practice of a Church of England Man* (1688) was written in the face of the new threat to that Church, this time from a Catholic resurgence. But in the midst of a refutation of Catholic claims, Stanley argues the purity of the Anglican Church against the nonconformists as well, attempting to convict the sects of schism while defending the Church of England from the same charge. In the end, his desire for a Christian unity extending even to the Eastern Church, though not to Catholics, is sufficient to make him openly renounce all claim to temporal penalties in the Church's discipline. While Anglicans are confident of "being in the right, . . . yet [we] dare not condemn absolutely all that differ from us."[43] Like Taylor and Allestree before the Restoration, Stanley looks to the gentry for religious leadership, calling upon them to "countenance religion" publicly and urging them to introduce religion into their discourse (pp. 75, 99–100, 170).

Two expansions of the Church Catechism were popular in the period after the Revolution. John Williams's *A Brief Exposition of the Church-Catechism* (London, 1689) had ten times as many questions and, though it was ostensibly for children, it seems more an elaboration of theological terminology than a practical guide. There is a noticeable attempt to be precise in philosophical definition, and although Williams took swipes at several Catholic positions, he is careful to use enough of the Dissenters' phraseology to avoid awakening any issues on that flank.

Zacheus Isham's *The Catechism of the Church: With Proofs from*

42. William Beveridge, *Of the Happiness of the Saints in Heaven,* in *Works of . . . William Beveridge,* 2:570–71, 566.
43. Stanley, *Faith and Practice,* pp. 4, 8–9, 17–19, 193.

the New Testament (London, 1694) multiplies the number of questions sixfold and is simpler than Williams's and more suitable for children. It is largely given over to the scriptural "proofs" or texts which justify Anglican belief and practice.

The balance of the later best sellers were short Anglican devotional treatises. William Howell's *The Common-Prayer-Book the Best Companion In the House and Closet As well as in the Temple* (1686) consists of prayers, some from the Prayer Book and others in the new fashion of "ejaculatory prayers," as well as lists of sins of omission and commission such as those included in several other Anglican works. Such lists, using the Ten Commandments as a general outline, were to guide in self-examination before communion and offer something like an inventory of the social ethics and manners of the time, including prohibitions on abortion, usury, duels, unlawful war, and deceitfulness in business.[44]

Finally, there is Sir William Dawes's *The Great Duty of Communicating Explain'd and Enforc'd* (1699), written for his own parishioners when he instituted a monthly communion. It does not appear that more frequent communion was occasioned by their demand so much as by his idea of their duty, since so much of the pamphlet was given over to answering the familiar objections against attending. It is fitting that the last of our best sellers should have been taken up with the problem of indifference.

The most obvious observation about this Restoration religious literature is that it was purposely written on a popular level. Not even the Countess of Morton pretended to be writing only for her private use or that of her family, and none of the works were technical treatises on theology, history, devotion, or controversy which just happened to attract a wider audience. All of the authors saw their purpose as the modest but serious one of admonition and encouragement.

To this end most of them adopted a plain expository style, though several of the Puritan writers used an exclamatory and emotional approach with obvious associations with the Psalms. The works by laymen—Themylthorpe, the Countess of Morton, and Penn—do not stand out by any greater familiarity of style. Those books designed

44. William Howell, *The Common-Prayer-Book the Best Companion In the House and Closet As well as in the Temple*, 3d ed. (Oxford, 1687), pp. 87–102.

primarily for young people—by Ken, Patrick, Brookes, Richard Sherlock, Williams, and Isham—were written on virtually the same level as the rest, although they did show some concern for that group's special needs. Allestree, in *The Decay of Christian Piety* and *The Gentleman's Calling*, showed a thorough mastery of the witty, paradoxical style then fashionable, and of course Bunyan's work was a more imaginative achievement than the rest.

For the most part, very little originality was shown in the choice of imagery, Scripture being the main source of illustrations as well as of arguments. Allestree employed a wealth of metaphors from law, business, agriculture, warfare, and even chivalry, in his more modish books. The most obtuse of his gentleman readers could have understood his point when asked, "Will a man renounce a rich unchargeable Reversion, when he is not only wooed, but bribed by a considerable Sum in hand not to disclaim it?"[45] And Allestree shared with Brookes an enthusiasm for classical history and legend and for the fabulous lore in Pliny's natural history. William Sherlock, writing for lawyers, showed that he could move easily in the realms of science and business. Calamy, too, liked analogies drawn from science or the naturalists, although they sometimes went awry: "The *Moon* is never in the *Eclipse*, but when the earth comes between us [*sic*] and the Sun."[46] Comparisons of the Christian life to warfare or pilgrimage appeared as early as Thomas à Kempis and as late as William Sherlock, though in the latter's urbane discussion they seemed incongruous.

Some of the authors recognized the difficulty of finding appropriate figures. In using what was surely the oddest source for imagery, the Koran, both Allestree and Smith apologized for employing a mere fable.[47] But it did contain a picture of heaven, and describing heaven was, as Hart complained, like holding a candle to the sun.[48] Bayly, whose imagination was the most equal to the task of representing death and the afterlife, expressed the wish to wean readers from inadequate figures, like that of God as "an old Man sitting in a chaire."[49] But here was a problem, for while Bayly and others (especially Dissenters) were trying to draw their readers away from this world, there was a dearth of symbols with which

45. *Gentleman's Calling*, p. 153.
46. *Godly Mans Ark*, sig. A8v.
47. Allestree, *Causes of the Decay*, p. 5; Smith, *Great Assize*, pp. 152–53.
48. *Christ's Last Sermon*, sigs. B5v–C2.
49. *Practice of Piety*, p. 46.

to represent any other. Their sense of the past was too weak for an escapist evocation of the world of Jesus' ministry or that of the Old Testament. Bunyan's allegories solved the problem of representation, but only a few allegories can be effective in any generation. The eventual solution lay with the didactic novels which replaced these religious works as manuals of conduct by furnishing providential plots with realistic detail.[50]

Examples of actual Christian heroism or sanctity were quite infrequent and were all drawn from Foxe's memorials of the Marian martyrs, by Bayly, Smith, Calamy, Baxter, and Mead.[51] Obviously, it was the Dissenters to whom these martyrs meant the most. Beveridge was the only Anglican to honor their memory, in asserting that the grace evidenced by their endurance was proof of the inspired character of their reform of England's Church and liturgy.[52] The one jarring note was struck by Brookes, who repeated an episode in which Cranmer and Ridley used "carnal arguments" to plead with Edward VI to allow the Lady Mary to hear mass, until the young king burst into tears and they withdrew in guilty embarrassment.[53]

There was very little in the books that would strike the modern reader as having come from an unfamiliar folk culture. The witches, prophecies, portents, prodigies, apparitions, and magic that contributed to the chapbook literature were absent from these books, with the exception of the instances cited from Hart. Themylthorpe's early work contained the tale, also in Holinshed, of the sun's standing still for three hours while the Earl of Ormonde led Henry V's forces against Omor Arthur.[54] Otherwise, the world view presented would have made perfect sense to an Englishman living in 1800, and indeed many of the books were printed well into the eighteenth

50. See J. Paul Hunter, *The Reluctant Pilgrim* (Baltimore, 1966), pp. 19–22, 207–8.

51. Bayly, *Practice of Piety,* pp. 600, 666; Smith, *Great Assize,* pp. 349–51; Calamy, *Godly Mans Ark,* pp. 73, 107, 217; Baxter, *Call to the Unconverted,* p. 526; Matthew Mead, *The Almost Christian Discovered,* 16th ed. (Boston, 1742), p. 19.

52. *Excellency,* p. 561.

53. Thomas Brookes, *Apples of Gold for Young Men and Women: and a Crown of Glory for Old Men and Women,* 13th ed. (London, 1678), pp. 200–201. The story came from Foxe; see *The Acts and Monuments of John Foxe,* ed. George Townsend, 8 vols. (New York, 1965), 5:700–701.

54. *Posie of Godlie Prayers,* pp. 5–6; Raphael Holinshed, *The Chronicles of England, Scotland, and Ireland,* 3 vols. (London, 1586), 2:76.

century. There were no physical descriptions of the Devil, for instance, and references to witchcraft, while not unknown, were brief and theoretical, as though the writers had no personal experience of such matters. The only real surprise is that their geographical horizon had hardly widened since medieval times, as we can see from their recurrent use of the Prayer Book's phrase "Jews, Turks, Infidels, and Hereticks" to describe the outer sphere of mankind with which Christians hardly needed to concern themselves. Allusions might be made to the heathen in order to shame a morally degenerate England, but knowledge of the Indians (Hindus?) seemed limited to the fact that they worshipped the Devil.[55]

As to the major subject divisions—intellectual basis, God, self, and society—the popular works were agreed in making man and his soul the primary interest, categories relating to self accounting for half of all recorded themes. The amount of attention paid to God was greater than that paid to society except in the earlier best sellers, which were still occupied with the social disorders of the mid-century. Dissenters and Catholics found society of less interest than Anglicans did, neither being in a position to impose their polity. But only the Liberal works were significantly at variance with any of the groups of books in their distribution of interest, giving much greater attention to problems of intellectual authority.

On the simplest level of analysis, then, there was substantial agreement on the major subjects of religious concern. The later works were shorter and less colorful than those popular earlier. But most authors had never considered a decorative style or quaint matter necessary to their business of explaining the fundamentals of the faith, showing men their happiness to be in God's service, or exhorting them in their duty toward their neighbors.

55. Taylor, *Holy Living*, p. 54; Allestree, *Whole Duty*, p. 255; Allestree, *Causes of the Decay*, p. 26; on the Hindus, Alleine, *Alarm to Unconverted*, p. 93.

4. Sources of Intellectual Authority

It appears that in the period of the Restoration religious beliefs and doctrines were changing less rapidly than the assumptions and authorities which underlay them. For in the most popular religious literature the greatest differences to be registered over time concerned philosophical authority. There was no extended discussion of these matters, and such scattered comments as there were accounted for only 3 per cent of all codings. But it was the area in which popular authors were becoming noticeably more wary in their arguments and more discriminating in their choice of authorities. Anglicans and Dissenters did not differ in this regard; the charges that Dissenters were Old-Testament-minded proved not only false but meaningless. The two groups faced the same difficulties in an increasingly secular culture. And both showed an increasing tendency to avoid this area, since the controversy of "reason" versus "authority" had not turned out to be at all clear-cut.

In 1696 John Toland betrayed the exasperation of the more unsophisticated of the rationalists, who, having undermined the concept of revelation, found his own presuppositions in question: "It appears to me very odd, that Men should need Definitions and Explanations of that [i.e., reason] whereby they define and explain all other things. . . . The word *Reason* is become as equivocal and ambiguous as any other; though all that are not tick'led with the Vanity of Singularity, or Itch of Dispute, are at bottom agreed about the Thing."[1] The problem Toland tried to wave aside has not gone

1. Toland, *Christianity Not Mysterious*, p. 8. See also pp. 21, 31–32, for his attacks on scepticism and cultural relativism.

away, and the equivocal status of reason is still a problem to the sociology of knowledge. For the difference between reason and authority is commonly that between those parts of the ruling ideology which are still latent and secure, and those assumptions which are rising into consciousness and beginning to appear arbitrary.

In the earlier part of the century, John Ball had counted on the authority of social consent to guarantee that of revelation itself. The Bible, he asserted, was proven to be the word of God by the testimony of the Church, by the miracles which confirmed its prophecies, by its antiquity, and even by its literary style or styles, all of which were self-evidently divine "without all argumentation or furniture of perswation." In comparison with classical literature, parts of the Old Testament "in varietie and force of eloquence, doe farre exceed all authors, Greeke & Latin, . . . [so that] you may easily discerne, the one was written by a Divine, the other by an humane spirit." Like all seventeenth-century writers, Ball disparaged an "implicit faith," but whereas "things doubtfull may be proved, . . . things in themselves most cleare and certaine, be above all proofe and reason." And the authority of Scripture fell into this category of self-evident truths not amenable to demonstration.[2] Thomas Brookes, writing in the 1650s, could still assume that his readers would agree that "All other Books cannot equal Gods, either in Age, or Authority, in Dignity, or Excellency, in Sufficiency or Glory. *Moses* is found to be more ancient and more honourable than all those whom the *Grecians* make most ancient and honourable."[3] It was enough that the authority of Scripture was obvious to most Englishmen; any proof would do because none was really necessary.

In the eighteenth century an "Old Bailey theology" would put the New Testament writers on the witness stand to defend the historical fulfillment of prophecy and the miracles which established Christ's authority. But in the closing decades of the seventeenth only our Liberal authors, Nye, Locke, and Toland, were giving serious attention to these historical proofs. Meanwhile, the dignity and excellency of Scripture had begun to seem less self-evident to the "moderns" in English society. Nye must have sensed this change; he defended the elegance, wit, and poetry of Scripture against the assertion that it was too rustic and ungrammatical for a cultured sensibility. The authority of the past was still such that he thought

2. Ball, *Short Treatise*, pp. 7–19, 30.
3. Brookes, *Apples of Gold*, p. 210.

it worthwhile to assert that the Bible was "much the Ancientest Book in the World."[4]

In the popular works Scripture (category A1) was the most frequently mentioned source of religious knowledge, followed by nature and reason (A3), tradition (A2), and more distantly by special intimations of the Spirit (A6), and proofs from history (A5) including prophecies and miracles. Anglican and Dissenting works showed little difference in this ranking, the former having a predictably greater interest in the Church's traditions, the latter in history and special revelations. Popular authors made no distinction between nature and reason as sources of knowledge, the most common allusion being to the existence of conscience. Even John Hart's simple tracts made a typical appeal to the light of nature, in the assertion that the excellency of man's nature argued that he "was created for greater things than these here below."[5] And his sweeping reference to the "books" of God's Revelation, of Nature, of History, and of Conscience, as emanating from one Creator and harmonizing in one message, was in the most confident vein of the literature.[6] The earlier works did not argue these matters in detail. Ball referred to proofs of God's existence, as first and final cause, from conscience and "the consent of nations," and from the historical success of the Church.[7] Taylor was a little more explicit, describing what he took to be the "True natural religion, that which was common to all nations and ages. . . . That there is one God; that God is nothing of those things which we see; that God takes care of all things below, and governs all the world; that He is the great Creator of all things without Himself: and according to these were framed the four first precepts of the decalogue." Christian moral doctrine, he asserted, "is nothing else but the law of nature, and great reason."[8] References to reason were usually more casual, as when Allestree scorned to appeal to "implicit faith" in the Bible to persuade readers of "the great propriety and fitness" of its commandments.[9] He was the only popular author to allude to the shortcomings, rather than the normative position, of the early church, as if to show that the apologist need not be bound to traditional authorities.[10]

4. Nye, *Discourse*, pp. 190–96, 128, 178.
5. Hart, *Christ's Last Sermon*, sig. B2.
6. Hart, *Black Book*, pp. 1–5.
7. Ball, *Short Treatise*, pp. 2, 42–46.
8. Taylor, *Holy Living*, pp. 171, 43.
9. Allestree, *Gentleman's Calling*, p. 59.
10. Allestree, *Causes of the Decay*, pp. 368–74.

Books written after the Restoration did not display the same confidence in this range of authorities. Matthew Mead, who could be expected to show the least trust in man's natural capacities, sourly remarked that the very wisest of the ancients—naming Seneca and Quintillian—knew nothing of original sin. But even he hoped it would be allowed that human nature itself acknowledges "a God, and that this God must be worshipped and served by the Creatures."[11] The list of beliefs which were thus assured was growing shorter. Howell mentioned only the existence of God and man's duty of worship as truths "generally discovered to the most brutish Heathens by the mere light of nature."[12]

No author liked to think that he was taking his stand on "authority"; even in addressing the most humble audience Rawlet appealed to his readers as reasonable men, challenging them to show wherein the religious life was not "highly reasonable and for your own benefit."[13] But on the other hand, popular authors did not seem to want to discuss natural philosophy at any length. William Sherlock's attempt to demonstrate the immortality of the soul from nature seemed self-consciously audacious. His argument formed part of a general theodicy which was the only extensive treatment of natural theology in the popular literature.[14] In fact, it was the only development of doctrine in these books that would have seemed at all novel to a well-read contemporary. And it is suggestive that it is a justification of God before man's tribunal, the harbinger of a new era in theology. Sherlock had accepted the principle that man is the measure of all things, whereas other popular authors had not.

Such extensive argument was one sign of a growing defensiveness. There was a more widespread decline in references to reason or nature, history, and special revelations in the later period, and a corresponding rise in appeals to Scripture until it was mentioned more often than all other sources combined. The fear that freethinkers might use "reason" and "nature" against revealed religion was forcing writers to discriminate between the sources of doctrinal authority and to fall back on the surest resource.[15] These other

11. Mead, *The Almost Christian*, pp. 99, 82.
12. Howell, *Common-Prayer-Book*, sig. A2.
13. Rawlet, *Christian Monitor*, pp. 5, 13, 17, 31.
14. William Sherlock, *Practical Discourse*, pp. 90–110.
15. An apparent increase in attention to tradition in the later period was due to Stanley's long argument against Catholicism. Otherwise this category too showed a decline.

sources had always been subject to some slight scepticism, but they came more and more to be ignored as the intellectual basis of popular religion shrank. The popular literature, therefore, gives evidence of a general decline or contraction of Christian belief which was not limited to those who affected a fashionable and morally convenient atheism, as authors frequently suggested.

The treatment of Scripture by popular writers reflected a literary education which raised them above the crudest literalism. Ball explained that not everything in the Bible was to be understood or believed in the same way, and that, while it contained all true doctrine, some parts were only "amplifications" of the necessary doctrines. Arguments over the human authors, "this or that Scribe or Amanuensis," were the province of scholarship and not of faith. Ball was aware of the crudeness or apparent "foolishness" of Scripture from the standpoint of a philosophical mentality. But part of the proof of the Bible's uniqueness was the very absurdity of some of its commandments, prophecies, and promises, which no man who wanted to be believed would have invented, but which had been triumphantly confirmed or fulfilled in history.[16] William Stanley acknowledged "seeming Difficulties, and Contradictions" in Scripture but thought they were "chiefly, or only, in small and indifferent cases, which concern not the Essence of our Religion." He could hardly have been unaware that his argument against Papal infallibility was equally applicable to a Biblical literalism—that even an infallible authority would be useless without an infallible understanding, and that the words and the context of revelation were themselves ambiguous.[17] By his time, the sufficiency of Scripture, as much as its infallibility, was the issue.

It should not be supposed that authors lacked confidence in the Bible; the use of proof texts was universal, and there was a reckless confidence in proofs by analogy with Old- or New-Testament episodes. Nevertheless, in the very choice of Biblical citations one can see that Scriptural authority was becoming problematical. Books popular in the earlier period exhibited a close balance of Old- and New-Testament references, though of course the Old Testament is over three times longer. But later authors cited the New Testament three times as often as they did the Old. This was the only one of our typologies which registered a change over time at the highest

16. Ball, *Short Treatise*, pp. 9–10, 16–18, 26.
17. Stanley, *Faith and Practice*, pp. 23, 31–35.

level of significance, supporting the contention that it was in the area of intellectual authority that minds were changing most rapidly. The difference between our Dissenting and Anglican authors in this regard did not prove significant. Dissenters did not favor the New Testament as decisively as did Anglicans, but they could hardly be called "Old-Testament-minded" with all that that is thought to imply. They did not accord the Old Testament even a majority, let alone the three-fourths of their references which would have resulted from a random selection. An even greater proportion would have been necessary to show a positive favoritism toward that section. Certainly Anglicans invoked the analogies of baptism with circumcision, of the kings of England with the kings of Judah, and of their ministers with the Jewish priesthood, as much as or more than did Dissenters.

It has been said that even the devotional literature of the early seventeenth century showed a "very great preponderance" of attention to the Old Testament, reflecting the strenuous character of religion in that heroic age.[18] The Reformation was, after all, often viewed as a national struggle, analogous to the history of Israel. And a study of the sermons preached before Parliament in the critical years of the Civil War gave evidence of this association; three-fourths of the opening texts were from the Old Testament.[19] In this light, the decrease of references to all parts of the Old Testament and the increase in attention to the New would support the characterization of the Restoration as a period of religious retrenchment, as men found less use for the drama of God's intervention in history and more need of the lessons of spiritual inwardness. Such a climate would foster the growth of pietism within established religious and social forms, which is indeed the story of eighteenth-century religion in England, including the birth of Methodism.

There were numerous suggestions as to the parts of Scripture which were most profitable for certain age-levels and tasks. Simon Patrick mentioned the Psalms as especially valuable, and longed for the times when the common people sang them at their work, down

18. Helen C. White, *English Devotional Literature* [*Prose*], *1600–1640* (Madison, Wis., 1931), pp. 190–91; cf. Benjamin Nelson, *The Idea of Usury,* 2d ed. (Chicago, 1969), pp. 132n54, 243–44, on the supposed Hebraism of the Reformers.

19. John F. Wilson, *Pulpit in Parliament; Puritanism during the English Civil Wars, 1640–48* (Princeton, 1969), pp. 148–51. Wilson did not keep an account of references other than the sermon text.

to "the very children in the streets." He thought children enjoyed the drama of the Old Testament histories most, but was anxious to have them move on to the New Testament and especially its moral teachings. For the doctrinal and historical sections were often obscure, were not absolutely necessary to be known, and might safely be left until more mature years.[20] Bishop Ken suggested that children read the histories and gospels, as the parts easiest to understand.[21] But Taylor advised against making the histories any part of one's devotions, perhaps thinking that the Puritans had found them too stirring. He advocated reading the New Testament and the "Sapiential books of the Old, viz., Proverbs, Ecclesiastes, &c. because they are of great use to piety and to civil conversation."[22] Allestree enjoined the memorizing of Psalms for use as ejaculatory prayers, and Lake advised reading one chapter daily from Psalms and another from either Proverbs or the New Testament.[23] The tendency in this advice to suggest a division of wheat from chaff is carried further in Calamy's list of references prescribed for specific afflictions, and in his recommendation to make a collection of God's promises from the Bible.[24] The exhortations to mark in one's Bible carried readers further toward the creation of a private Scripture.[25]

In general, the Pauline epistles proved the favorite sources in this popular literature, accounting for more than a quarter of all citations. They were followed by the Gospels and the Writings (Job through Song of Solomon), each with a fifth, the rest of the New Testament (Acts, non-Pauline epistles, and Revelation) and the Prophets, each with about a tenth, the Pentateuch (6 per cent) and the Histories (4 per cent), while references to the Church Fathers, creeds, and councils amounted to less than 3 per cent of all references. The apocryphal Scriptures were almost completely ignored. In relation to the actual length of the various sections of Scripture, the relative advantage of each of the briefer New Testament sections was even more striking, and the Writings fell to fourth place.

20. Patrick, *Book for Beginners*, pp. 625–28.
21. Ken, *Manual of Prayers*, p. 11.
22. Taylor, *Golden Grove*, p. 612; Taylor, *Holy Living*, p. 165.
23. Allestree, *Whole Duty*, p. 419; Lake, *Officium*, p. 84.
24. Calamy, *Godly Mans Ark*, pp. 110–14, 146–48; see also Ken, *Manual of Prayers*, p. 68.
25. G. B., *Weeks Preparation*, p. 51; Allestree, *Whole Duty*, pp. 53, 442.

There was a surprising consensus in the above ranking. Anglican preference followed it exactly, while among Dissenters the Prophetic books were favored above the New Testament group containing Acts. Anglican authors referred to the Pauline writings more often than did Dissenters, and they also gave more attention to the Gospels. The suggestion that Puritans read the Psalms and Proverbs more than any other part of Scripture and were for that reason especially susceptible to Unitarianism and to the compensatory ethic and the resentment characteristic of this Old-Testament rationalism, seems at least questionable.[26] For the popular Dissenting works actually cited these sections less frequently than did the Anglican, and much less than they did Paul's epistles or the Gospels.

Only a handful of authors referred to sources other than Scripture or the Fathers, though a few—particularly Bayly, Brookes, Taylor, and Allestree—did so repeatedly. Among the ancients, Aristotle was invoked in seven of the books, Plato and Plutarch in five, Cicero and Seneca in four, and the ancient naturalists and poets were a frequent source of illustrations. But even the authors most addicted to classical references sometimes showed little sympathy toward their sources. While giving Socrates credit as a martyr for monotheism, Mead questioned whether his stubbornness was truly for God's sake or out of vainglory.[27] Plato was quoted as saying, after reading the first chapter of Genesis, "This man saith many things, but proveth nothing."[28] And the history of Julian the Apostate continued to be a caution to children, when the fatal arrow from Heaven forces him to concede that "thou Galilean hast overcome me."[29]

Augustine was easily the favorite of all the Fathers, particularly among Dissenters. And Dissenters were more likely to cite both medieval theologians and Protestant reformers. Brookes, Bayly, Pearse, Calamy, and Mead all mentioned Bernard, and several of them quoted Aquinas, Anselm, and Bonaventura as well. Continental reformers loomed larger than English ones. Five of our authors appealed to the authority of Luther, four to Calvin, three to Erasmus

26. Max Weber, *The Sociology of Religion*, trans. Ephraim Fischoff (Boston, 1963), pp. 111–12; idem, *The Protestant Ethic and the Spirit of Capitalism* (1904–5; rpt. New York, 1958), pp. 123, 165; H. John McLachlan, *Socinianism in Seventeenth-Century England* (London, 1951), p. 334.

27. Mead, *The Almost Christian*, p. 62.
28. Calamy, *Godly Mans Ark*, p. 66.
29. Brookes, *Apples of Gold*, p. 97.

and Melancthon, and the humanists Valla, Pico, Vives, and Grotius were also mentioned. Of Englishmen, only Foxe, Latimer, Jewel, Hooker, and Perkins were cited as authorities.

Contemporary philosophy was not discussed in the most popular religious literature, aside from allusions by Allestree to Machiavellians, Utopians, and a Leviathan state.[30] Even the most erudite of the authors were not entirely abreast of intellectual currents; three years after the publication of Newton's *Principia*, Bishop Beveridge still spoke of the tides as one of nature's impenetrable mysteries.[31] A few authors continued to draw the traditional lessons from the peculiarities of the dragon, satyr, unicorn, and phoenix.[32]

While Anglicans and Dissenters shared a common orthodoxy as regards intellectual authority, Catholics, Quakers, and Liberals differed markedly from them. These matters were actually the major theme of the Liberal works, where the claims of reason and Scripture were carefully weighed, and tradition discredited. Only our Liberals dismissed all special revelations as "enthusiasm." Quakers, on the other hand, favored personal revelation, if we may so designate the Inner Light, over even Scripture, while rejecting reason. Standing outside the stream of English culture, the Quakers were especially likely to see reason as the comfortable assumptions of dominant groups. Catholics appealed to these sources of authority rather indiscriminately. And they seemed the least aware of a crumbling intellectual consensus within Christendom, as can be seen in their neglect of the duty of belief (F3). This was a major theme among the best sellers (4 per cent of paragraphs), especially in the early period. Quakers and Liberals discussed belief even more often than did the popular authors.

The choice of Scriptural citations showed a similar pattern. Catholic books were impartial in their choice of references, striking a balance between Old and New Testaments. They did not favor St. Paul as did the others, referring to his epistles less often than to the Gospels and Writings. Quakers closely resembled the popular writers in their use of Scripture, and Liberals strongly favored the New Testament, especially Paul, and almost ignored the Writings, which, as poetry, could not have been of much use in their argu-

30. Allestree, *Causes of the Decay*, pp. 300, 263, 240, 352, 226.
31. Beveridge, *Happiness of the Saints*, p. 569.
32. Taylor, *Holy Living*, p. 23; Smith, *Great Assize*, p. 161; Allestree, *Gentleman's Calling*, pp. 3–7, 94.

ments. In short, Catholics seemed the most devotional and Liberals the least, if we can judge from their choice of Biblical references.

But with reference to the larger typology of Old- versus New-Testament emphasis there is some question whether it signifies anything beyond itself. An orientation toward the Old Testament did not have the expected correlations with the other typologies of religiousness which we can construct from our subject-matter categories. An Old-Testament emphasis was actually related to the more benign image of God. The only significant, if puzzling, correlation was with a relative naturalism as opposed to supernaturalism. Beyond this, there were positive but nonsignificant relations between an Old-Testament orientation and the following: an ethical understanding of religion, a neglect of God, activism, anxiety, and a sectarian bias. All of these were emphases characteristic of the earlier period.

Besides the question of the sources of religious knowledge, there is the matter of the degree of confidence that was shown in that knowledge. Recognition of mystery or paradox at the heart of Christianity (A8) was a very weak theme, though it grew more common. The contrary position, that man's religious knowledge could be infallible, was hardly entertained at all. Curiously, though, it came to much the same thing; authors made the routine admission of the obscurity of things, confident that nothing of importance was left to be guessed at. The notion of a progressive development in religious knowledge (A9) was virtually unknown in the popular literature, though Penn and the Liberals Nye and Toland entertained the thought.

Among our popular authors, only the Anglicans suggested that the essentials of the faith were few and that vital doctrines were clear enough in the words of Scripture itself (A7). But they did not suggest that the distinction between essentials and "things indifferent" allowed for liberalism. In fact this anti-intellectualism was related to authoritarianism. In the past the distinction had been used to force compliance with the stand of the established Church on inessentials. For the more doctrines that could be classed as inessential—not endangering one's salvation—the broader would be the area in which conformity could be demanded and coercion applied in the interests of ecclesiastical decorum.[33] That Dissenting authors ignored the doctrine may indicate the success with which

33. Croft, *The Naked Truth*, p. 19, attacks this interpretation.

it had been turned against a liberal interpretation. Liberals Toland, Croft, and Locke did attempt to draw out the anti-authoritarianism implied in the distinction, but among the best sellers it was the more intellectually authoritarian which alluded to the doctrine most often, perhaps out of its long association with compulsion.

Finally, there is the question of how useful the labels "liberal" and "authoritarian" are in characterizing popular works in this period of shifting philosophical allegiances. Our typology of intellectual authoritarianism was constructed from categories expressing the value of tradition, Scripture, and objective proofs from miracle and prophecy, the certainty of man's religious knowledge and the dangers of heterodoxy and unbelief, to show a commitment to a traditional intellectual order. More liberal books, besides avoiding or rejecting the above, were identified by their emphasis on nature and reason, on the possibility of private discoveries and further development in religious knowledge, and on the dangers of ignorance, superstition, and formalism.[34] Scripture, of course, has often been used for the "prophetic" purpose of breaking the hold of traditional thinking and challenging a "culture" or "folk" religion which has become a mere reflection of social mores. After periods of scholastic rationalism, a return to Scripture may have a liberating effect, intellectually and spiritually. It appears, however, that if the generations prior to the Restoration erred it was in the direction of too pronounced a Biblical literalism, so that an insistence on Scripture must have seemed entirely traditional.

While Anglican and Dissenting books showed no appreciable difference along this authoritarian-liberal dimension, works popular in the earlier period were markedly more authoritarian than later ones. But in only two of the works was discussion of intellectual authority a major theme—in Stanley's argument against the Catholic Church and in Allestree's treatment of The Causes of the Decay of Christian Piety. The group of Quaker works proved significantly more liberal than any others, while the books by recognized Liberals showed the most pronounced authoritarianism. This anomaly may be explained by the fact that Liberals were very much more interested in questions of authority than were other authors. In the course of lengthy discussions, Liberal authors had to make clear where they stood in relation to more traditional sources of authority

34. Intellectually authoritarian/liberal (A1, A2, A5, A8, I18, I19/A3, A6, A9, I16, I17).

and were glad to show where these supported them. It turns out that, in terms of the total attention to these themes, Catholic works most frequently side with traditional authorities.

Of course, even "nature and reason" can be used as an external authority to establish a cultural orthodoxy. The line between nature and that "second nature," custom, is indistinct, and so it is in the interest of the established orders to appeal to "nature." It has already been argued that "reason," used to mean truth and not simply logical consistency, is socially determined. On the other hand, Scripture can be used to challenge conventional assumptions as well as to buttress them. The popular literature did not, however, indicate that this was the case in the late seventeenth century. The specific categories of reason and Scripture were equally correlated with social authoritarianism, but the relation was not significant. There was, however, a significant relation between intellectual authoritarianism and social authoritarianism. There were also significant correlations between intellectual authority and a "churchly" as opposed to a sectarian mentality, and with a neglect of self—correlations that underline its close alliance with social authority.

Authorities are challenged by other authorities. Dissenters, who were slightly less authoritarian than Anglicans intellectually, were significantly more liberal in the matter of social authority but significantly more authoritarian religiously, on a measure described in the next chapter. They had found a basis outside the customs and assumptions of their day. The correlations between social and intellectual authority and their negative correlations with this religious authoritarianism[35] suggest the possibility that religion—with its claim to transcendence—would ordinarily show more independence from the pervasive influence of convention than would other forms of thought. Indeed, the religious basis of so much social and cultural change is one of the questions that brought modern sociology to birth.[36] It is interesting in this regard to compare the use which various groups made of the prophetic books of the Old Testament, the most notable challenges of this kind. As might be expected, Quakers invoked them most often, whereas Liberals ranked them next to last. Dissenters, too, were almost three times as likely to cite

35. The negative correlation of religious and social authoritarianism was significant, while that between religious and intellectual authoritarianism was not.
36. See H. Stuart Hughes, *Consciousness and Society* (New York, 1958), p. 284.

them as were Anglicans. Insofar as the prophets represented a con-
demnation of existing institutions, Liberal authors again appear to
occupy a conservative position, and on the measure of social authoritarianism they did, in fact, fall between Anglicans and Dissenters.
An emphasis on the prophets had significant correlations with a
social liberalism and with categories representing Weber's "prophetic" as opposed to "traditionalist" religion.

In short, while popular Anglican and Dissenting works present
a striking agreement on questions of religion's rationale, the choice
of authorities, and the use of Scripture, there was a noticeable
development from the earlier to the later part of our period in these
matters. First, there was a slight decline in attention to matters of
intellectual authority at just the time when these were becoming
a major concern in more specialized theological works. Further,
there was a decline in reliance on sources other than Scripture at a
time when other lines of appeal were being explored by what are
usually taken to be influential thinkers. No doubt these changes
are to be interpreted as suspicion of other supports rather than as
a sign of growing confidence in the Scriptural basis of the faith.

In the growing differentiation of Scripture from other authorities,
and in the singling out of New-Testament, and especially Pauline,
citations as more suitable to contemporary audiences, the works
register a certain embarrassment over elements of religion which
were coming to be recognized as old-fashioned. The Bible was
ceasing to be read as a whole. Authors were more careful not to
outrun their warrants, and the admission of obscurity and paradox
in the faith was becoming more frequent. In all of this, we see a
growing awareness of the isolation of Christian belief from the
nation's intellectual life.

5. God, History, and the Supernatural

Industrialization is often taken as the process that destroyed the animistic or supernaturalistic world of our ancestors. But a century before England's industrial revolution, the notion of supernatural agency had already been much simplified and the area of the sacred reduced. If the Restoration was a transitional period as regards its theological foundations, it was more like a dead spot in the history of the religious spirit. For the dread of God and of the powers of evil declined markedly in popular literature before the process of "humanizing" the image of God had well begun. The prophetic, historical sense of the early reformers had largely disappeared without being replaced by any hope of earthly progress.

We have already seen that popular religious literature devoted less space to discussion of God than to discussion of self. On the other hand, God's disposition and expectations were a more constant theme than society. And yet, even the most devotional of the works conveyed very little of the sense of the numinous which would have given this interest some flavor. Anglicans complained that the Puritans lacked any feeling for the holy, as in Beveridge's complaint that "together with the Liturgy, they laid aside all Distinctions betwixt sacred and common things; by which means the whole Nation was in danger of being overspread with Prophaneness and Irreligion."[1] Allestree expressed the same horror at Puritan sacrilege in taking the endowments intended for religious uses and in stabling their cavalry in God's churches.[2] But only Hart seemed overcome by shock at the blasphemous impostors of the Interregnum or the

1. *Excellency*, p. 562.
2. *Whole Duty*, pp. 46, 99–106.

increasing profanation of the Lord's Name and His Sabbath. Our other authors reserved any indication of a sensitivity to the holy for discussions of God Himself. For Dissenters this had begun to take the form of an affective but impotent mysticism, while the Anglicans' piety became somewhat more rational and mundane.

Only six of our works failed to mention the power of Satan, but a personalized evil was an infrequent theme (B12—1.5 per cent of paragraphs). There were no circumstantial tales of Satanic activity except those we have noticed in Hart. The Devil was hardly more personified than Mammon or Envy, and was normally treated as synonymous with temptation. Baxter alluded to a collection of case histories of demonic possession he had gathered for the purpose of convincing atheists, but he treated them as little more than ontological specimens.[3] If there was a more exotic literature on this subject at the time, it was not among the most popular reading matter of the day.

Belief in the demonic was secure, but interest in the subject appears to have been declining. Works with an early popularity, and especially those by Hart, had shown the greatest concern. He blamed Satan for the growth of antinomianism and efforts to "beat down Magistracy and Ministry, which is the great work the devil aims at, that so he may the more easily delude Souls."[4] At the other extreme, Allestree treated the theme almost jocularly in his *Decay of Christian Piety*, convinced that most of the evils he complained of were the result of human malice. And Vincent's work, in the same early period, was one of the few that made no mention of Satanic activity, even in a discussion of the calamitous Plague and Fire. Still, it is a measure of the certainty of belief in the Devil that one of the earliest authors could appeal from his existence to that of God Himself: "By the assaults and suggestions of Sathan we feele there is a Devill, may we not then certainly conclude that there is a God? . . . why should hee seeke Gods dishonour, and mans destruction, if there were not a God, a law, and an everlasting life."[5]

Only six books mentioned witches or mediums (B13). And among those who cautioned against practicing spells or curses or resorting

3. *Call to the Unconverted*, p. 506; see below, chapter 7.
4. Hart, *Christ's First Sermon*, sig. C2ᵛ; idem, *Plain Mans Plain path-way*, sig. A4.
5. Ball, *Short Treatise*, p. 46.

to witches, wizards, sorcerers, or charmers it was never clear that they believed in the efficacy of these activities.[6] Calamy supposed that the appearance of Samuel at the bidding of the Witch of Endor was only an apparition of Satan's devising.[7] Even Taylor, whose three paragraphs on witchcraft led all the books, showed little curiosity about the subject. Only he, with his particular interest in sexual purity, was prompted to mention the Devil's fornication with witches.[8]

Angels, too, were almost entirely absent from the best sellers (B11). Only Themylthorpe took for granted the presence or the need of "thy holie Angell."[9]

But the figure of God dominated the literature. Indeed, He loomed so large that the dimensions of the subject could hardly be made out. There was little abstract discussion of the nature and attributes of the Godhead (B3), and it amounted only to metaphysical compliments. The catechumen learned that "God is an infinite, Eternal, and Incomprehensible Being, having all Perfection in and of himself."[10] A historical qualification—"the God of Israel" —seemed awkward and quaint; the image of God could not be specified or differentiated for readers who were overpowered by a sense of His reality.[11] They did not need to be told what it meant that He was man's Maker, Redeemer, Sanctifier, Creator, Owner, Ruler, Benefactor, Father, Lord, and King.[12] In this regard, as in others, the books were written to remind readers more than to inform them.

God's Fatherhood, so interesting to psychologists of religion, was not a matter of precise definition. Williams thought that the title was appropriate "as he created all things." But Ball made Him "our Father by grace and adoption," and not, apparently, by nature.[13] Perhaps the separation of many or most children from their fathers, as orphans, bastards, apprentices, boarding scholars, or servants, would explain the vagueness of this image. Though no count was

6. Ibid., p. 182; Bayly, *Practice of Piety*, p. 550; Allestree, *Whole Duty*, pp. 62, 277, 442; Ken, *Manual of Prayers*, p. 24; Rawlet, *Christian Monitor*, p. 46.
7. *Godly Mans Ark*, p. 102.
8. *Holy Living*, pp. 57, 206–8.
9. *Posie of Godlie Prayers*, passim.
10. Williams, *Brief Exposition*, pp. 10–12; Isham, *Catechism*, p. 13.
11. Richard Sherlock, *Principles*, p. 31.
12. Baxter, *Call to the Unconverted*, pp. 543–44.
13. Williams, *Brief Exposition*, p. 11; Ball, *Short Treatise*, p. 116.

taken, the title of Father did not seem to compare in frequency with the terms Lord and God; it was left to the hymn writers of the next century to enlarge the stock of names for God.[14]

Much has been made of the Puritans' fear of God. It is true that some of the books by Puritans and Dissenters presented an image of a vengeful God which is scarcely to be found in the Anglican writings. Smith's *The Great Assize* frequently returned to the theme of Christ's coming in judgment, precipitated by numerous offenses among which Sabbath-breaking came first to mind.[15] Baxter's book was written in the shadow of a God Who could barely contain His wrath. And Doolittle, who was no more than orthodox in his view that it is impossible for the natural man to please, much less to satisfy, a righteous God, added a note of petulance in the need to remind God continually of Christ's satisfaction for sin. For He is "*a God of infinite jealousie,* and he is most jealous in the matter of his Worship. . . . If there be but one among a thousand that receiveth unworthily, his eye will be upon him" and his "damnation will be aggravated."[16] And Mead thought God played upon the fears even of His elect, to keep them striving for assurance.[17]

Among Anglicans, Taylor did declare that God often defers answering our requests because He loves to hear men beg.[18] But he never pictured God as peevish or as a figure of genuine terror. William Sherlock might carelessly assert that God could turn us "out of our earthly Tenements at pleasure," but he never doubted that a justification of God's dealings could be made in terms that would satisfy his audience.[19] Allestree expressed the gravest objections to the distinction which Mead had implied, between God's apparent revelation or His intimations, and His secret mind. He asserted that those who believed that God played false even with His elect would not scruple to use deceit in His service.[20]

It is curious, therefore, that when Allestree tried to account for the decay of piety in his time he twice attacked the Puritans' over-

14. See Samuel Rogal, "Watts' *Divine and Moral Songs for Children* and the Rhetoric of Religious Instruction," *Historical Magazine of the Protestant Episcopal Church* 40 (1971):95–100.
15. Pp. 9, 21, 225.
16. *Treatise*, pp. 40–43.
17. *The Almost Christian*, p. 107.
18. *Holy Living*, p. 179.
19. *Practical Discourse*, p. 200; for his theodicy, see pp. 90–110.
20. *Causes of the Decay*, p. 164.

confidence—their emphasis on God's mercy and the satisfaction of Christ to the neglect of man's duties.[21] But certainly Dissenters could be as warm in their descriptions of God's love as Anglicans, despite their apprehensions. Smith himself assured his readers that "What good thing soever the heart of man can wish or desire, that will God bee unto us. If thou desire wealth, God will bee it unto thee: If honour, if pleasure, Almighty God will be all in all unto us." And Baxter, too, asserted that God took no pleasure in condemning men, but only in their conversion.[22] Russell thought that God might "terrifie thee with Judgments," but only as He would also "allure thee with Mercies," in order to produce a proper seriousness in spiritual matters. And Calamy, who had quoted the Proverb describing God's mockery of the wicked in their destruction, elsewhere enlarged on the benevolence of God, likening His promises to "the breasts of God, full of the Milk of Grace and comfort."[23] In fact, there was more affective mysticism in the Dissenters' best sellers than in those by Anglicans, as will appear in reference to the figure of Christ.

Nevertheless, when those categories showing the sterner side of God's nature were combined and contrasted with others showing His benevolence, the Dissenting works did prove to give a harsher view of God on the whole.[24] The typology showed a greater difference over time, however. The severe image of God in the earlier works varied significantly from the benign representation in the later books and in the perennial best sellers, perhaps one of the reasons that the latter retained their favor. The fear of God did not show the expected correlations with conversionism, the Old Testament, or a general authoritarianism, but there were significant relations with anxiety, activity, and an "ethical" (as opposed to sacramental) religion. Among individual writers, the reasons for religious dread are far from clear. Bunyan, Mead, Calamy, and Penn, all writing under difficult circumstances, showed less apprehension than the later Anglicans Rawlet, Williams, and Dawes, possibly indicating a connection between fears for social order and a harsh

21. Ibid., pp. 168–72; idem, Whole Duty, p. 9.
22. Smith, Great Assize, p. 215; Baxter, Call to the Unconverted, p. 509.
23. Russell, Seven Sermons, p. 147; Calamy, Godly Mans Ark, pp. 68, 218, 150, 27, 122–23.
24. Stern/benevolent God (B1, B4–5, B12–13, C1, C4, D4, F2, F7, F9, I14, J5, J7/B7–11, C2–3, C5, D10, F1, F4, F8, J4, J6). The difference between Anglican and Dissenting works was not significant.

image of God. For there was a significant relation of this severe image with an interest in society if not with social authoritarianism, and no apparent correlation with sectarianism, itself a threat to that order.

The image of a personal God is necessarily anthropomorphic, and will change along with the prevailing view of man. The Restoration did bring a new awareness of the variety of human feelings and responses which was soon to be reflected both in the novel and in a "humanizing" of God. There is no evidence from this study that religion was becoming more man-centered.[25] But the figure of God was more humane and less awe-inspiring in some of the later Anglican works. No doubt this was part of the development from what religious historians have called "piety" to "moralism," with God depicted less as master and more as helper. In time, God was to become little more than a father, or even a grandfather, existing to promote His creatures' happiness.[26]

One way in which this humanizing process might have proceeded would have been by greater attention to Christ. Locke's *The Reasonableness of Christianity*, one of our group of Liberal works, portended the separation of the figures of Son and Father which would open the way for a greater curiosity about the historical Jesus and for a more sentimental devotional tradition. But more typical of the best sellers was a confusion concerning the persons of the Godhead: "Come Lord Iesu, from thy Kingdome of Grace, to thy Kingdome of Glory: and not for any merits or deserts of mine, but for the Lord Iesus Christs sake, who is the Sonne of thy love."[27] Professor White thought that she noticed a shift in emphasis from the Son to the Father as she proceeded from the devotional literature of the fifteenth century to that of the sixteenth.[28] Our works would bear out the common contention that during the Reformation period the focus was on the figure of the Father. There is little difference if one compares the space given to the person

25. Attention to both God and Christ rose slightly while that toward man remained constant from the early to the later best sellers. But the works with a constant popularity were higher in attention to all three subjects, while neglecting social and philosophical questions.

26. Joseph Haroutunian, *Piety versus Moralism: The Passing of the New England Theology* (New York, 1960), pp. 137–45; C. F. Allison, *The Rise of Moralism* (London, 1966), passim.

27. Smith, *Great Assize*, p. 299.

28. White, *Tudor Books of Private Devotion*, p. 246; *English Devotional Literature*, pp. 194–95.

and work of the Father (B1–7) as against that of the Son (C1–6) in the divine plan. But when the duties of man toward God were spelled out (F1–9) the authors directed attention specifically to Christ in less than a tenth of the instances, though it is not always clear whether or not the title Lord was meant to denote a particular person of the Godhead.

Most of the interest in Christ was still concerned with his official roles rather than with any personal attributes. And that of atoning sacrifice (C1) was more prominent than all others combined, which were (in order) lover or friend (C5), teacher and example (C2), judge (C4), and finally the incarnation and revelation of Deity (C3). Anglicans were more likely to give attention to Christ's teachings (C2), while Dissenters emphasized his love and judgment (C5, C4). But Anglican and Dissenter agreed on the primacy of the atonement.

All of the affective mysticism in the literature was directed toward Christ. Calamy's Mrs. Moore spoke of being "deeply in love" with Christ and panting after the "altogether lovely" one. She was "thirsty after Jesus Christ" and felt her soul "transplanted into Christ."[29] Pearse longed for "full Embraces in Christ's Bosom, full Views of his Face," which may be psychologically associated with his theme of affliction and persecution.[30] Even the frightening Doolittle thought it was a sin to go to communion with "dull affections," and so tried to "inflame" the worshipper with a meditation on "Twenty Properties of the Blood of Christ": "Oh! lay your heart a steeping in this blood, and try if it be not *softning blood*. . . . Oh! then bring your dead heart, and dull affections to the Blood of Christ, it will quicken and enliven them, for it is an enlivening blood." Then, "When you come unto a Sacrament, the great God is to come into your heart, therefore set open the everlasting gates of your Soul, that the King of Glory may enter in: And let every room in your heart be washed and cleansed, and hung with the Tapestry, and Embroidery of the Spirit."[31]

Anglicans did no more than match these effusions. The *Weeks Preparation* viewed the sacrament as an aid in "weaning the senses from sin to devotion" by feasting them on Christ's love. "He made himself my meat, and my drink, to enter within me, for which cause

29. *Godly Mans Ark*, pp. 239–48.
30. *Great Concern*, p. 161.
31. *Treatise*, pp. 72–93, 49.

I am to hold his pains as mine own. . . . O that I could enter into
his enflamed heart, and see the furnace of infinite fire, that burneth
therein, and melt in those flames."[32] Lake drew guilt and devotion
together: "As *thou* didst not disdain to be entertained even in the
house of SIMON the Leper; as *thou* didst not reject the *Harlot*, a
sinner like unto me, coming unto *thee* and touching *thee*; as *thou*
didst not abhor *her* foul and profane mouth . . . admit *me* also, an
overworn, miserable, and out of measure *sinful* Creature to the . . .
saving *Mysteries* of *thy most holy Body* and *precious Blood*."[33] And,
despite Taylor's cautions to seek only the duty and conscience and
not "deliciousness and sensible consolations in the actions of religion," he himself encouraged communicants to put their "lips to
His fontinel of blood, sucking life from his heart."[34]

But these are all of the more heated examples; the normal tone
in describing Christ's nature or work showed the same respect or
awe with which the Father was treated. Only a few of the books
suggested a more humanized image. In the context of the other
popular works, Taylor's phrase "our elder brother" seems too familiar, almost jarring.[35] Ken's use of Jesus as an example of one who
had overcome the temptations common to youth is also too human,
probably, to have seemed quite in character then.[36] And Penn's
concentration on the example rather than the death of Christ must
have raised some eyebrows.[37] Few as they are, these were presages
of the changing vision of God which characterized the next century's pietism.

The Holy Spirit was not a subject of interest in its own right, and
what little mysticism the literature expressed was not associated
with the person of the Spirit. Even regarding its role in man's spiritual birth and development (D10), the Spirit of God was discussed
barely more often than Satan in popular religious works.

A concentration on God and Christ was perceptibly higher in the
Anglican best sellers than in those by Dissenters. But again, it was
highest in those books with a long-term popularity and lowest in
the early period, though even this difference was not statistically
significant. The correlations of concentration on God and on Christ

32. G. B., *Weeks Preparation*, pp. 18–19, 75.
33. *Officium*, p. 67.
34. *Holy Living*, pp. 185, 218.
35. Ibid., p. 239; idem, *Golden Grove*, p. 627.
36. *Manual of Prayers*, pp. 7–8.
37. *A Key, opening the Way*, pp. 784–85.

were the same and suggested a passive, confident, and sacramental religion, as well as a neglect of the subject of society. There were less marked but still significant relations between an emphasis on God and the more benign image of God and, oddly enough, with a general anti-authoritarianism. In short, those seventeenth-century works which concentrated their attention on God were those which showed the most confidence in life.[38]

God's guidance of human affairs was universally assumed in the popular literature, but it was not expected that dramatic or miraculous violations of nature would ever be common. God used second causes and hid His hand within history, so that the dozens of rather ordinary providences that readers might remember or expect in the course of their lives might be recognized only by the eye of faith. Authors routinely asserted the Creator's power over His world and His determination of the course of history (B4, B7). But these were never meant to preclude human freedom or providential adjustments within a rather general plan. None of the works discussed even predestination theologically—from God's point of view—but only in reference to the individual's curiosity, so that we may defer it to the next chapter. The use of dreams, lots, or fortune-tellers to divine a predetermined future may have been common then. But only Lake mentioned it, as vain and superstitious.[39]

On a practical level, the discussion of God's governance bore on the question of whether sickness, poverty, or other afflictions were providential or natural. Fourteen of the books and over a third of the references to sickness (G8) at least hinted that it might be a judgment on sin, although several of the same books denied that the connection held true in all cases. Six writers made no such associations in their discussion of sickness. And, in reference to poverty (G9), the providential connection seemed less clear. Twelve books spoke of economic adversities as judgments or trials, though again some of the same works admitted that this was not invariably so. Sixteen books indicated no such connection, nor did the great bulk of references to poverty.

It was relatively easy to account for economic distress in terms of human failure, and writers suggested philanthropies to meet real

38. Emphasis on Christ also correlated significantly with social liberalism and with supernaturalism. Emphasis on God (B1–8, C1–6, D4, D10, F1–9). Emphasis on Christ (C1–6, and those codings of F1–9 which referred specifically to Christ).

39. *Officium*, p. 114.

affliction. But in reference to illness there was little that men could do. Bayly only thought to recommend physicians as preferable to magic.[40] Writers fell back on the fact that the only real cures were spiritual, as Howell implied when he instructed that "every friendly Visitor should endeavour to excite . . . remorse and sorrow for his former sins" in the hapless invalid.[41] After all, God would allow adversity only in an effort to humble man and bring him into dependence. So, while these troubles might be punishments, they were assuredly also opportunities to purify one's faith and devotion. Indeed, trials were to be a source of comfort, showing God's concern with one's spiritual maturity. They helped to wean man from this world. And what was this world but a source of analogies for the pains of hell, from a burning city to toothache.[42] As Calamy observed, our afflictions "are evidences that wee are in a blessed condition" and "teach us to know God *Experimentally* and affectionatively, not *cerebraliter* (as Calvin saith)."[43] Anglicans would have concurred.

It did not tax the ingenuity or faith of the seventeenth-century reader to come to terms with misfortune religiously. Only William Sherlock, before an audience of lawyers, felt obliged to remark on the moral problem of human mortality. But then, life on earth had become sufficiently miserable since the Fall to make "the greatest part of Mankind have . . . no temptation to wish it longer."[44] Apparently the public did not demand a justification for God's providence that went beyond man's own responsibility and an eternity of recompense. To have dissociated God from human misery by intermediate causes would not have solved the moral difficulty and would have robbed adversity of its religious meaning.

Perhaps with the Dissenter Pearse, who was probably dying as he wrote, we begin to see afflictions being valued for their own sake, seemingly apart from any role in the development of firmer character or a more spiritual devotion. As the expectation of persecution stretched indefinitely into the future, it seemed to him that

40. *Practice of Piety*, p. 550.
41. *Common-Prayer-Book*, p. 44.
42. Ibid., p. 38; Bayly, *Practice of Piety*, p. 555; Calamy, *Godly Mans Ark*, pp. 8–22; Pearse, *Great Concern*, pp. 114, 125–27, 181; Smith, *Great Assize*, p. 65.
43. *Godly Mans Ark*, pp. 10, 29.
44. *Practical Discourse*, pp. 100, 135.

"to be wholly free from all Personal Affliction, and yet greatly to lay to heart, and be afflicted for the Afflictions of God's Name and People, this is glorious Grace, Grace in lustre." The glorification of suffering as an end in itself became a prominent theme in eighteenth-century Evangelicalism.[45] By then Evangelicalism had less excuse, in that it did not face the same persecution.

Reports of providential afflictions or guidance are commonly taken as evidence of narrow self-centeredness and stunted conceptions of God. But the amplitude of Restoration views of the Deity did imply that He must be everywhere if He is anywhere. Popular authors did not share the even more anthropomorphic notion, common later, that God may concern Himself with the whole but hardly with the parts as well.

Still, while they were awed by God's greatness and believed that His providences lay all about them, the idea of historical change was almost wholly absent in the popular authors, despite England's recent turmoil and the moral deterioration they deplored. God's covenants (B8) with Israel and the Church, and the promised Kingdom of God (B9, J4) were among the most neglected categories. And even these pointed to a distant future and a distant past. For the present, God might judge nations for wickedness or unfaithfulness but was not working toward any discernible goal within the world's process. Certainly He was not guaranteeing any advance of man's civilization.

The handful of references to the millennium all admit considerable uncertainty. Penn tentatively associated the doctrine with the Quakers' new way of peace and conciliation.[46] The latest of the Dissenting books seemed to place the new age outside history, convinced that the end of this world was near.[47] Sherlock surmised that the "thousand's years [sic] reign of the Saints with Christ, whatever that signifies," might simply be symbolic of the end of the reign of death, which had cut off even Methusaleh before his thousandth year.[48] Allestree went so far as to deny any Scriptural

---

45. Pearse, Great Concern, p. 114; E. P. Thompson, The Making of the English Working Class (New York, 1963), pp. 350–74.
46. A Key, opening the Way, p. 788.
47. Russell, Seven Sermons, pp. 240–44.
48. Practical Discourse, p. 129. Sherlock expressed himself doubtful that lunar cycles rather than years were used in reporting the ages of the patriarchs (p. 132).

warrant for the doctrine of a millennium, which had exercised such a pernicious influence among the enthusiasts of his day.[49]

Taken all together, these themes were dwarfed by comparison with the theme of the vanity and misery of the world (J1–2.2%). The Restoration of so many things in English life, however superficially, must have reinforced the idea that historical change was illusory. Popular literature appears to confirm the observation that the Restoration fell between the collapse of the hope for a world-shaking spiritual renewal and the expectation of an earthly and human progress.[50] We shall see that categories indicating a passive mentality showed up with increasing frequency while those theological components which are thought to have contributed to progressive-mindedness were weak and declining.[51] Only Stanley sounded the new note, in his expressed desire "to leave it [the world] *better than* I found it."[52]

Curiosity concerning the afterlife took the place of interest in the world's future, accounting for a seventh of all codings. Rewards and punishments in the afterlife remained the primary motive for performance of religious duties (E4) right into the later period. There was some change in emphasis over time, from judgment (J5) and hell (J7) to the second coming and resurrection (J3) and heaven (J6), putting a more hopeful face toward the future. The greatest differences in this regard were not over time, but between Anglicans and Dissenters. Death itself (J2) was a major theme of the nonconformists' literature while among churchmen it was not. Contrasts over the second coming and judgment also show the Dissenters' greater interest. And, if Anglicans were nearly as likely to discuss heaven, Dissenters were far more apt to mention hell. Belief in hell was too secure a part of general culture to argue a psychological projection or even a sour disposition in the believer; men as sensible as the Jesuit Parsons, the Dissenter Russell, and

49. *Causes of the Decay*, p. 368.

50. Grierson, *Cross-Currents*, p. 329.

51. The passive/active typology is described in the next chapter. Ernest Lee Tuveson identifies neo-Pelagianism and moral improvement, mystical ascent, Christ as teacher, and the primacy of reason over revelation as conducive to the idea of progress, with emphasis on tradition, the Fathers, and imputed righteousness as detrimental: *Millennium and Utopia* (Berkeley, Calif., 1949), passim. Of the relevant categories, A1–3, D2–5, and the Fathers were moving in the wrong direction, B7 and F8 were static, and only C2 and G3 were contributing to greater progressive-mindedness.

52. *Faith and Practice*, p. 56.

Bishop Beveridge could blandly agree that most men, even most Englishmen, would likely be damned.[53]

Dissenters found themselves living in another world from Anglicans. A typology designed to polarize themes involving this supernatural realm and a more naturalistic cast of mind showed that the decline in supernaturalism over time was slight compared with the difference between popular Dissenting and Anglican works.[54] Differences within the groups were wide enough for the Dissenters' supernaturalism not to prove significantly greater. But the correlations of a supernaturalistic emphasis suggest the importance of the other world to those who had no assured place in the present one. There were significant relations with sectarianism, an emphasis on self and a lack of social interest, and with a rejection of social authority and religious traditionalism. It is not surprising that a rejection of this world should be correlated significantly with a conversionist piety and a passive temperament. The significant relations of supernaturalism with emphases on Christ and the New Testament are more curious, perhaps indicating the source of this spiritualized piety. Finally, supernaturalism was related to a religious authoritarianism.

This religious authoritarianism embraced those categories which indicated God's unaccountability to man or which recommended humility. "Religious liberalism," on the other hand, described a melioristic view of human life and a more comfortable relationship with God.[55] And here Dissenters varied significantly from Anglicans. Their greater authoritarianism on this measure contrasts with their comparative liberalism in the areas of social and intellectual authority. And the significant correlations with this mentality emphasize that clash of authorities, indicating an anti-traditional, sectarian, socially liberal stance, a neglect of society and emphasis on self. Contrary to expectations, religious authoritarianism's correlations with a stress on God and with the harsher image of God were negative (and nonsignificant). It was significantly related to anxiety and conversionism. Religious authority was obviously the founda-

53. Parsons, *Christian Directorie*, p. 116; Russell, *Seven Sermons*, p. 8; Beveridge, *Happiness of the Saints*, pp. 564, 572.

54. Supernaturalism/naturalism (A1, A5–6, A8, B4, B11–13, C1, C4, D2, D4, D10, E4, G4, G8, I3, I7, J1–7/A3, A9, B4–10, C2–3, D1, D3, E3, E5–8, G3, G9, H3, I1, I10–13).

55. Religious authoritarianism/liberalism (B4, B11–13, D2, D4, E4, F7, F9, G4–5, G8, J1–2, J5/B7–9, D1, D3, E3, E5–6, F8, G3, G9, J3–4).

tion under those who were unable to fall back on traditional social or cultural supports.

Catholic, Quaker, and Liberal groups sometimes offered a striking contrast to the best sellers in these matters of God's nature and influence. Of all our groups, the Catholic works presented the most kindly image of God, and showed the least interest in Satan and the greatest interest in angels. They also were the most insistent on the misery of this life, and devoted the greatest attention to heaven and hell. Quaker treatments of God tended to be theoretical rather than devotional, and consequently lacked warmth. Quaker writers were also curious about the nature of Christ, emphasizing his roles as judge, as the incarnation of God, and as teacher, much more than did the best sellers, and stressing his atoning death somewhat less. Their interest in the Holy Spirit was, of course, pronounced.

For Liberal authors, the consideration of the nature of God was second in importance only to the question of the basis of religious knowledge. Quite predictably they were the least supernaturalist and the most likely to discuss natural causes (B7), and they were the only authors to express an interest in the wonders of creation (B10). Biddle, at least, insinuated doubts as to Christ's divinity, while the others stressed his roles as judge and as teacher.

The only surprise in all this was the similarity of Quakers to Anglicans, and Catholics to Dissenters, in relative emphasis on God, supernaturalism, and religious authority. For want of a better explanation, the resemblance between Catholics and Dissenters might be put down to the earlier dates of composition of many of the Catholic and Dissenting or Puritan works.

The treatment of God and supernatural agency suggests rather different conclusions from those we reached in considering the intellectual basis of religious doctrine. For regarding the latter the greatest differences were registered over time and not between ecclesiastical parties.

It is true that the books popular just following the Restoration gave the least attention to God, Christ, or Holy Spirit, and stressed the Father's most fearsome side. But it was not those with a later popularity which represented the opposite pole in these respects. Rather, it was the group of those with a continuing popularity, some of them among our oldest works, which were at the other extreme and which emphasized the more gratifying of man's duties to his Maker.[56] This was also the group that showed the least curiosity about God's governance of the world, however, and the group that tended most to emphasize the woes of this life (B4, J1). In short, they were the most devotional of the books, in their concentration on the bonds between man and God and in their avoidance of theological and moral difficulties. Works popular after the Revolution, on the other hand, gave more attention to questions of the abstract nature of God and Christ (B3, C6) than did other best sellers. Evidence of the growth of this more theoretical interest is supported by the decrease in interest apparent in the categories of the love and fear of God, Satan, and the vanity of the world. Popular literature, then, suggests a change from religious engagement in a time of turmoil to detachment after the Revolution. Yet the market for an earlier, more devotional literature did not slacken through this period.

With the more general attitudes of religious authoritarianism, emphasis on the supernatural, and emphasis on the afterlife, however, the greatest differences were not those caused by changing circumstances but those that divided nonconformists and churchmen. The Dissenters' emphasis on both the love and fear of Christ (C4, C5) showed a greater fervency of spirit, as against the greater curiosity among Anglicans concerning Christ's nature and example (C2, C6). In short, more of the Dissenters' emotional energy was bound up in another world.

Their Puritan forebears had not thought of this world as futile, but rather as the stage upon which God displayed his wisdom and power. After ecclesiastical failure and political defeat, however, it was only natural for the doctrine of His providence to shrink from a historical to a personal scale. God's designs proved deeper than the Puritans had bargained for. Not that these authors despaired of knowing God's will, but that will was increasingly identified with individual moral considerations rather than teleological ones. The prophetic awe at the historical spectacle was fading.

In time, this historical sense would be rekindled by the hope of an earthly progress. The distance that separated the popular works from those by Liberals shows that this naturalistic faith had not yet touched the general public. But this public was not indifferent to

56. See the next chapter for the treatment of F1-9.

the charge of superstition; it was one of their own shibboleths. Though James II's court might go in for miracles, the reading public could be justly described, like Sir Isaac Newton himself, as "supernatural rationalists."[57] For, while naturalism was not yet a possibility, the desacralizaton of history and institutions was already well advanced.

57. See J. R. Western, *Monarchy and Revolution* (London, 1972), pp. 209, 268; McLachlan, *Socinianism*, p. 11, borrows the phrase "supernatural rationalism" from Adolf Harnack.

resolution are able to effect" that stimulated these Anglicans to try to awaken some industry and responsibility in an indolent Anglican gentry.[67] *The Whole Duty of Man* did associate assurance and diligence in a prayer to "make me some way useful to others, that I may not live an unprofitable part of mankind; but, however, O Lord, let me not be useless to myself, but grant I may give all diligence to make my calling and election sure" (pp. 430–31). And Lake included a similar prayer that God would make his "*Calling* and *Election* sure; make me in some measure *useful* to my self and others, both as to *This*, and a *better life*." The fact that these men never brought themselves to mention calling and election otherwise may indicate that they were offering a commonplace. For these associations with a Calvinistic election were not authentic; Lake next prayed for help "to hold out unto the end, that so I may be saved."[68]

Some still spoke of diligence in one's calling as the duty to reconcile oneself to a birthright position rather than as a means of bettering one's circumstances.[69] The moralistic authors were the most open to the possibility of upward mobility (H10). Rawlet, who at some times insists that "God knows what Condition is best for us," softens that teaching with the hope that godliness may help one rise out of poverty at least. Even the "meanest sort" live more comfortably when they are sober and "diligent in their callings."[70]

Again, it should not surprise us that this sense of the efficacy of man's work should be found in those authors who were most insistent on human freedom and the building of character. The puzzle, as Weber recognized, is how to explain the activism of those who believed God to be the source of character change, and the indolence of those who had always been told to work for their salvation. The case of our semi-Pelagian authors offers its own explanation: where moralism was not combined with a real reliance on the sacraments, these moral duties were the way to God's favor. Dissenters, meanwhile, searched their devotion and sentiments for assurance.

67. Allestree, *Gentleman's Calling*, sigs. A4ᵛ–A5; Allestree, *Causes of the Decay*, p. 35; Taylor, *Holy Living*, pp. 9–16; idem. *Golden Grove*, pp. 613–17; Stanley, *Faith and Practice*, pp. 147, 160–61; William Sherlock, *Practical Discourse*, pp. 164–66.
68. *Officium*, pp. 129–30, 133.
69. Themylthorpe, *Posie of Godlie Prayers*, p. 27; Douglas, *Daily Exercise*, sig. B12; Isham, *Catechism*, p. 56; Williams, *Brief Exposition*, pp. 40–43.
70. *Christian Monitor*, pp. 38, 53, 20.

Popular authors showed little sophistication or interest in discussing the proper motivations for religious dutifulness. The simple injunction to obey God (F2) was given as much space (7.6%) as were all discussions of motive. Anglicans, who offered to discuss motives more than did Dissenters, mentioned rewards or punishments in the afterlife (E4) most often, followed by happiness or mental well-being (E6), reputation (E8), material well-being (E5), the disinterested desire for righteousness or the attraction of virtue (E3), and last, the good of society (E7). It should be noted that they ordinarily rejected reputation as a worthy motive and expressed doubts about material advantage as well. They were also more likely than Dissenters to reflect that common prudence reinforced godliness (D3).

Dissenters gave even more space to the afterlife as a motive, and appealed to a disinterested virtue more often, but to mental well-being considerably less, than did Anglicans. They were entirely scornful of reputation and material prosperity as motives in religious duty, and did not mention social well-being.

The contrast over desire for happiness as a motive is revealing. Popular Dissenting works devoted far more space than those by Anglicans to the theme of the blessedness of the righteous and the woes of the ungodly (D6–7), these being among their most common themes. But they treated happiness as a product of right-standing with God, while for Anglicans it was held out as an incentive to achieve that standing. Perhaps the Dissenters' use of godly sorrow as a mark of the elect was a reaction to the feeling that others were using happiness as the ulterior goal of their religion.

The difference, which seems wide in a theoretical sense, may have been unimportant practically. For whether happiness was used as a sign of the elect or an inducement to godliness, either might suggest an instrumental religion in which spiritual duties were valued as means toward self-regarding ends. The public may have read the same message in either party's works. Schneider and Dornbusch have pointed out the "paradox of instrumentalism," in that the instrumental value of religion seems to depend on the conviction that it has more than instrumental value.[71] When alternative paths to the true goal are found, an instrumental piety will fall into decline. But the Dissenters' treatment of happiness as a by-product and not the end of religion, and their relative neglect of worldly motives,

71. Schneider and Dornbusch, *Popular Religion*, pp. 64–77.

would make less likely the raising of these questions of instrumentality in readers' minds.

Certainly the charge that Dissenters were particularly open to "this-worldly" considerations goes against the evidence of their popular literature. Calamy and Doolittle ranked disinterested duty above even the afterlife as a motive, and several of the Dissenters were sensitive to the possibility that even hopes and fears regarding the afterlife might reveal a basic selfishness. The good man should be able to say that "If there were no Hell, yet I would not sin against the Lord."[72] With both groups, descriptions of the afterlife focused on spiritual joys and the pains of conscience, and were not dominated by the cruder physical imagery for heaven and hell.

Even in the Anglican literature, there is no evidence of a truly naturalistic ethics. William Sherlock adopted a hedonistic system, but depended on the fact that the pains and pleasures of the afterlife dwarfed those of this world. For he, along with other Anglicans, frankly admitted that only fear of hell would restrain men.[73] Of course, this would not have justified an appeal to eternal punishment if there had been any doubt of the existence of Hell. But the irony and hypocrisy that masked the doubts of philosophers about that doctrine were entirely foreign to the popular literature.[74] There was some feeling, as we have seen, that fear of punishment was a less pure motive than love or duty, but there was no hint that the fear was unjustified.

There was no change in attitude within this literature toward the more prudential motives. Restoration readers could not have failed to notice the pervasive instrumentalism of modern inspirational literature.[75] The bare assertion that self-interest reinforced piety did not go unchallenged by Dissenters.[76] For what was accepted as given was not the world, to be manipulated by whatever means religion might provide, but rather God's demands, to be met

72. Doolittle, Treatise, p. 160; E4 was sometimes coded negatively for Alleine, Bayly, Bunyan, Calamy, Doolittle, Mead, William Sherlock, and Thomas à Kempis.
73. Practical Discourse, pp. 244, 232–33; Allestree, Causes of the Decay, pp. 173–74; Patrick, Book for Beginners, p. 622.
74. See Walker, Decline of Hell, p. 187.
75. Schneider and Dornbusch, Popular Religion, pp. 12–18, 74.
76. Alleine, Mead, and Bunyan differed most notably from Allestree, Taylor, Rawlet, William Sherlock, and Dawes over the appeal to prudence (D3) and over the naïve conception of perfectibility implied in the general admonition to improve oneself in virtue (G3).

in the most conscientious manner they knew. Dawes was disconcerted by his parishioners' objection that they could not think of any good they had ever received from communion and could only retort: "Supposing no benefits at all were to accrue to us, from our receiving the Lord's Supper: What then? Are we to obey none of our Saviour's Commandments, but such as we are to be gainers by? Is it not enough that he has plainly enjoyn'd us to do this?"[77]

The authors were too scrupulous to use incentives that they recognized as strong, simply to bring religion back into fashion. Only Allestree, in *The Gentleman's Calling*, would admit that even unworthy motives might be useful at the first. Only he made any appeal to snobbery, in his attempt to discredit vice as plebeian and atheism as ignorant.[78] His attack on the killjoy theory of virtue, like Sherlock's supernatural hedonism, may have encouraged the view that the proper test of a religious doctrine is the human happiness it promotes. But it would be a long time before this utilitarianism would change the basis of religious authority. It may be that the wit and "sense" of these two works reached readers who would not have endured any of the other books. And their perspective may even have been adopted for this tactical reason. These were the only works which seemed to recognize and start from what actually motivated men, rather than from the recognition of God's demands. If the other best sellers were scarcely interested in man's proper motivation, they showed no interest at all in the causes of man's rebellion or of his unregenerate desires.

Moral casuistry, the resolution of ethical dilemmas, also received very little attention in this popular literature; indeed, the term "casuistical" was used pejoratively to connote sophistry and compromise. No doubt the Dissenters' silence shows their rejection of a temporizing moralism. It was Anglicans who provided the few examples of casuistry, taking seriously the questions that remained after Scripture had fallen silent. Allestree and Taylor expressed the need for "reason" and "natural law" as against an ethical rigorism.[79] Practically speaking, this might mean that a man concerned with moderation in eating should consider present customs, the company he is with and their educational level, "the judgment of honest and wise persons, and the necessities of nature." In dealing with ser-

77. Dawes, *Great Duty*, pp. 32–33.
78. *Gentleman's Calling*, p. 113, et passim.
79. Ibid., p. 59; *Holy Living*, pp. 116, 43.

vants, Taylor advised masters to go by the "contract made, by the laws and customs of the place, the sentence of prudent and merciful men, and by the cautions and remembrances given us by God." Sometimes he sounded more like a bourgeois apologist than a kindly country rector: "In judgments between the rich and the poor: it is not to be considered what the poor man needs but what is his own." His reckonings of restitution stipulate that "If I persuade my neighbor to commit adultery, I still leave him or her in their own power; and though I am answerable to God for my sin, yet not to my neighbor."[80] Allestree, on the other hand, mentioned the restitution due for fathering a bastard, at least in a penurious household.[81]

Patrick offered some guidance on the "Doubts and Scruples" of the young, particularly in regard to parental authority. Specifically, they must obey the commands of their parents if these are not contrary to divine commandments, and accept "their directions also about the choice of your calling, if you have not a natural aversion to it." This same subjection is important, "especially in the business of marriage, in which parents have always had a right to dispose of their children; not indeed to force them to marry one whom they cannot love, but to oblige them to endeavour to love those whom they recommend to their choice." Failing in this endeavor, children must still not marry without the parents' consent unless parents are unreasonable. And ordinarily they can be proven unreasonable only by a contrary judgment by magistrate or minister who should be asked to intercede. In general, his advice is to "use your liberty prudently," not trusting to personal "prejudice" in opposition to established usages.[82]

Several of the Anglicans appended lists of sins for guidance in confession, which could also serve as an elaboration of one's moral duty. They were more likely than Dissenters to mention the need for a continuing repentance (G5), presenting it as a satisfaction for the sin. The more Pelagian of the authors spoke of "*acting revenge* upon thy self by *Fasting*, and other acts of Mortification."[83] Taylor's rule was that there should be at least as much sorrow for

80. *Holy Living*, pp. 49, 130, 125, 133–39.
81. *Whole Duty*, p. 236.
82. *Book for Beginners*, pp. 618–21.
83. Lake, *Officium*, p. 117; Allestree, *Whole Duty*, pp. 136–37. For "heads of self-examination" see Lake, *Officium*, pp. 113–24; Allestree, *Whole Duty*, pp. 440–53; Howell, *Common-Prayer-Book*, pp. 87–102; Ball, *Short Treatise*, pp. 198–213; Ken, *Manual of Prayers*, p. 24.

the sin as there had been pleasure in committing it. And as a further attempt at restitution, as though Erasmus and the Reformation had never been, he suggested a form for making vows when in danger, leaving a blank for *"the sum you design for holy uses."*[84] For Dissenters, mortification of desires was a means of avoiding sin and creating a realistic humility, not an atonement for past guilt. They recommended fasting too, but for the health of the soul, not as retribution toward the body.[85]

In general, Dissenters were much more concerned with control of thoughts (G1–8.8%) than with control of actions (G2–4%) while Anglicans held a balance between these negative virtues (6.4 and 5% respectively), and were more outspoken than Dissenters about fleshly sins. The subjectivism of Dissenters can be seen in their greater attention to the duty of private devotions (G6). Doolittle's preparation for communion was entirely mental, in contrast to the preparation recommended in Anglican treatises, which dwelt on the most suitable demeanor and postures. And perhaps the closest thing to a casuistical judgment in the Dissenting literature was discussion of the unpardonable sin, which must be no less than a deliberate mental rejection of the Spirit after some experience of God's forgiveness.[86] Their introspection could reach paralyzing levels, as in Bayly's directions on humor: "If thou be disposed to be merry, have a speciall care to three things: First, that thy mirth bee not against *Religion*. Secondly, that it bee not against *Charity*. Thirdly, that it bee not against *Chastity*; and then bee as *merry* as thou canst, *only* in the Lord."[87]

Puritanism has come to mean a horror of the flesh and of sexual activity. It is ironic that in the best sellers this repugnance for carnality was expressed by the Puritans' bitterest enemies. Taylor's virginal ideal found no counterpart in the popular Dissenting works. Even between married partners, he would allow only affection; sexual intercourse was to be performed with all possible solemnity, as befitted temperate natures. For passion or "Sensual pleasure is a great abuse to the spirit of a man, being a kind of fascination or witchcraft, blinding the understanding and enslaving the will."[88]

84. *Holy Living*, pp. 207–8, 228.
85. Ball, *Short Treatise*, p. 167; cf. Taylor, *Holy Living*, p. 65.
86. Russell, *Seven Sermons*, pp. 18–19; Mead, *The Almost Christian*, pp. 65, 128.
87. *Practice of Piety*, p. 253.
88. *Holy Living*, pp. 63–64, 44.

Given this primacy of sensual instincts over the mind, it was natural that Anglicans should show greater concern with the flesh and use the terms of pollution and impurity for sin.

Indeed, our most Pelagian authors were often the most "Puritan." Only Allestree thought to object to Christmas merriment or to sports, as a waste of time if not worse.[89] And as to redeeming the time, the curse with which Puritans are thought to have blighted English society, the injunction was stated as forcefully by Anglicans.[90] It might be argued that Dissenting authors could assume this diligence in their readers. But, as stated earlier, these elements of the work ethic are easier to explain in the context of a moralistic religion than as Weber did it, as part of a Calvinist piety. Their pervasiveness in English society might better be put to the account of Anglicanism.

Man's duties toward God were a major concern of Anglican authors, who tended to treat the whole of religion in these terms. Simple obedience (F2) came first to mind, and then worship (F6), reliance or dependence (F4), love or thankfulness (F1), belief (F3), fear or humility (F7), the more negative command simply not to displease God (F9), and finally the wish for fellowship or union with God (F8). Any of these might be called "faith," a term which still had an unspecialized connotation.

Dissenters paid more attention to the questions of personal regeneration and justification than to these matters of duty. They also ranked obedience first among man's duties but gave it only half as much attention as had Anglicans. Beyond that, they differed only by emphasizing worship and dependence much less and the desire for fellowship somewhat more than did Anglicans. They saw a danger in thinking of religion in terms of one's duties, because such a religion could mask a hypocritical spirit. Mead's book was largely given over to the detection of feigned love, legalistic obedience, blind faith, presumptuous reliance, superstitious worship, and false humility. Where there was a proper gratitude the danger of legalism would not arise. Dissenters more frequently directed their religious duties specifically to Christ than did Anglicans, indicating, perhaps, that their duty was done from the motive of thankfulness more than to gain favor.[91] For Anglicans, who addressed their duties to

89. *Whole Duty*, pp. 51, 206.
90. Taylor, *Holy Living*, p. 14; Lake, *Officium*, pp. 107–9; Pearse, *Great Concern*, p. 71; Russell, *Seven Sermons*, p. 150.
91. Association of duties with the figure of Christ was highest in regard to

the Father, there seemed some question as to how far God might still have to be appeased.

Finally, in overall interest in categories concerning man or self, the popular Dissenting works held a wide lead.[92] The gap between them and Anglicans, while not statistically significant, was the widest between any of the groups of books. And the correlations of this emphasis are what one would expect of a Dissenter's attitude: sectarian and anti-traditional, neglectful of society, religiously authoritarian and socially liberal, supernaturalistic and active.[93]

Occasionally the other groups represented the farthest extremes. Catholic works were the most moralistic, the most interested in motives and especially the afterlife (E4), the most insistent on watchfulness over one's actions (G2) but the least concerned with belief (F3). Quakers, by contrast, were the least concerned with motives and the most conversionist and active in tone. In the matter of anxiety, these groups fell between the popular Dissenting and Anglican books. Liberal works were not concerned with the nature of man or his duties toward God, except for the theme of belief. They were the most likely to cite the good of society as a motive (E7), reinforcing the appearance of social conservatism we have noticed in them.

Throughout this consideration of man's duty and happiness, no mention has been made of developments over time, since they seemed comparatively unimportant. As with questions concerning God and history, the widest differences were sometimes between the early favorites and the long-term best sellers. The former revealed the most anxiety, activism, and introspection (G1), were the most interested in some considerations of motive (D3, E4–5) but least interested in the various religious duties (F1–8) and in devotional exercises (G5–7). The latter were at the other extreme in all these regards, demonstrating that the more devotional works wore better.

We know from other evidence that a moralistic piety was gaining ground. In the 1690s the newly tolerated Dissenting sects were rocked by controversy over the posthumous publication of Tobias

---

thankfulness, fellowship, and reliance (F1, F4, F8), lowest in regard to fear or the desire not to offend God (F7, F9).

92. Emphasis on self, man (D1–10, E3–6, E8, F1–9, G1–9, H7–8, I13, J2, J5–7).

93. There was also a significant correlation with intellectual liberalism.

Crisp's predestinarian treatises, written before the Civil War. In the moralistic atmosphere of the later period, Crisp's works were stigmatized as antinomian.[94] For the Dissenting clergy were being affected by the Arminian or Pelagian tendencies which we noticed first in Taylor's works. Judging from their popular literature, the main body of Dissent had perhaps not moved as much with the times. Best sellers continued to speak in the terms of man's fallen nature and God's converting grace. Popular Dissenting works offered no very consistent position on the question of just how much depended on one's response or how one could be assured of God's favor. But the degree of agreement is striking when they are compared with the most popular Anglican works, which differed significantly both in their moralizing doctrine and in their greater self-confidence.

Anglican distaste for the elitism implied in election no doubt encouraged their clergy to turn to an emphasis on man's responsibility. For them, sin did not imply an entire estrangement from God and it could not be overcome in one crisis of spirit. Rather, it was the sum of one's commissions and omissions, and was atoned for in a lifetime of obedience and submission. There was a stoical quality in Anglican works that contrasts with the greater emotionality of the Dissenters. Their moralism hardly allowed a relaxation of effort in this world, whereas for Dissenters the joy of salvation was supposed to be a present possession. Indeed, the alternation of spiritual depression and exaltation in the Dissenters' works has been taken as one source of the melancholy sentimentalism of the next century.[95] For where sorrow itself was considered a sign of regeneration, the emotional life was easily brought to a pitch that grated on sober Anglicans.

It may be that the Church's laity resisted this moralistic piety, as did their Dissenting counterparts. There was little decrease among the conversionist themes in best sellers despite a decline in the number of popular Dissenting works. The latest of the Anglican books employed an evangelical terminology at least, though it may have done more to undermine Calvinist doctrine than the frontal assault.

Though popular religious literature might resist change with regard to the image of man, the moralistic doctrine noticeable in this

---

94. See Olive Griffith, *Religion and Learning* (Cambridge, 1935), pp. 94–105.
95. Hoxie Fairchild, *Religious Trends in English Poetry*, 5 vols. (New York, 1939–62), 1:220, 536–46.

literature would be advanced by the novels which were shortly to appear. A belief that man's character and destiny were in his own hands, a prerequisite for literary realism and the study of man, was implicit in the Anglican literature. The Dissenters' greater introspection would never have led to a fictionalized treatment of man, since it was God for whom they searched within man's soul. But Anglicans proved more interested in probing man's motives, reconciling his duties, and differentiating his sins. In time this new and broader interest in man, his bestiality and his benevolence, would alter the outlook of our civilization.

7. The Church and a Secular World

In the midst of medieval society, *The Imitation of Christ* had warned that the Christian should keep much to himself. He must avoid the company of the young, the rich, strangers, and women, and the hearing of "newes and tales."[1] With the religious reformations of the sixteenth century came the hope that the whole of society might come to meet higher standards of knowledge, devotion, and conduct, and achieve that spiritual unity that had proven so elusive in Christendom. But by the time of the Stuart Restoration that hope had faded, and for many English authors, both Dissenters and Anglicans, the old advice again seemed relevant to their own circumstances. Indeed, *The Imitation of Christ* was cited for its counsel to shun evil or frivolous company.[2] Both parties now believed that they formed islands in a sea of indifference or unbelief. And, as Dissenters were being driven back upon the family, so Anglicans began to think of religious societies for the serious-minded as bastions against a secularizing society.

Despite the fact that differences over social and ecclesiastical policy showed up the greatest differences in emphasis between popular Dissenting and Anglican works, few books argued these matters. However reluctantly, authors seemed willing to submerge their differences in order to face the greater threats of superstition and disbelief. Churchmen no longer took their stand on the state's power to compel religious conformity, but appealed to the beauty of the

1. Thomas à Kempis, *Imitation*, pp. 22–23, 58–59.
2. Taylor, *Golden Grove*, pp. 619–21; for similar advice, see Douglas, *Daily Exercise*, sigs. B12, C3ᵛ; Lake, *Officium*, pp. 17, 24; Patrick, *Book for Beginners*, p. 622; Stanley, *Faith and Practice*, p. 150; Rawlet, *Christian Monitor*, p. 51; Mead, *The Almost Christian*, p. 10; Russell, *Seven Sermons*, p. 217.

Church's services and the need for social agreement, to bring men back to Anglican allegiance. Dissenters had more nearly lost hope for English society.

The Puritans had been slow to acknowledge the implication of their religious stance—that they would always be minorities within the nation. The medieval Church had worried over an often profane society. But the profane had largely shared the world view of their Church, and it sometimes took only a spark to fire their devotion. Sectarianism, on the other hand, defined itself in opposition to a lost world for which there was no hope or even a point of contact. For some time sectarian reformers had expected to see greater liberty in religion lead to convergence of belief. But by 1660 it was clear that it was leading to greater divergence and even indifference. As the movement hardened into sects their attitude became one of resignation and resentment. They might exhort or evangelize their neighbor, but sometimes—like Bunyan's pilgrim confronting Talkative—it was more to clear themselves of a responsibility than with any expectation of success.[3]

Bitterness toward a scoffing world was a prominent feature of popular religious literature. The favorite of Jesus' parables was the story of the beggar Lazarus and the rich man, whose earthly circumstances were dramatically reversed in the afterlife (Luke 16: 19–31). Nearly all the Dissenters referred to the story, not for its contrast of rich and poor but to express a general resentment over their pariah status.[4] And the next in popularity, the story of the wise and foolish virgins (Matthew 25:1–13), bore much the same message: there is no way to awaken most people to consideration now, but those who have lived in indulgence here will be shut out hereafter and will envy those they now disdain. Anglicans showed a certain uneasiness with these stories, as when Rawlet improved on the text in insisting that Dives was damned not for being rich but for being "Luxurious and Proud" and Lazarus saved not because he was poor but because he was "a Pious Good Man." Allestree and Taylor concentrated on Dives rather than on the beggar, to encour-

---

3. Bunyan, *Pilgrim's Progress*, p. 82.
4. Bayly, *Practice of Piety*, p. 185; Smith, *Great Assize*, p. 69, et passim; Calamy, *Godly Mans Ark*, p. 30; Alleine, *Alarm to Unconverted*, p. 80; Mead, *The Almost Christian*, p. 136; Vincent, *Gods Terrible Voice*, p. 11; Pearse, *Great Concern*, p. 33; Baxter, *Call to the Unconverted*, p. 530; Russell, *Seven Sermons*, p. 37; Hart, *Christ's Last Sermon*, sig. A4ᵛ; Hart, *Black Book*, p. 20; see Weber, *Sociology of Religion*, pp. 110–16.

age readers to greater charity toward the poor.[5] There was still time, they hoped, to give the story a happy ending; Dissenters perhaps preferred it as it stood.

This may serve to symbolize an important party difference. Anglicans were not as likely to dismiss an ungodly society as beyond all help, feeling that the Church had some responsibility for the whole nation. For example, they expected to find enough common ground with the general reader to argue or shame him into agreement. Allestree thought that the current wave of vice might be reformed if gentlemen would only use their natural authority to commend Christian practice.[6] Others lamented the open licentiousness, the professed disbelief in God or providence, and the decline in worship.[7] But Anglicans thought much of this a pose and were most apprehensive of schism (I15) and heterodoxy (I18)—the sources of social division.

Dissenters were less troubled by the spectre of God's judgments on England (I14) than were Anglicans, so profound was their estrangement.[8] Vincent's treatment of the destruction of London suggests a feeling almost of vindication. He recalled a child whose only regret in succumbing to the plague was that he had not been spared for martyrdom instead, in the expected persecutions of Dissent. And he betrayed a certain satisfaction in the many who had been shaken out of their atheism during the plague, too late.[9] Only in reference to superstition (I17) and unbelief or indifference (I19) did Dissenters show slightly more concern over their society than did churchmen.[10] This was part of their general concern over matters of belief, noticed earlier, which may have been related to their own ideological insecurity.

But while the parties might differ on the kinds of fears expressed, the level of this concern differed most markedly over time. Starting with vice (I20), and including the other dangers just mentioned, books popular just after the Restoration showed by far the greatest

5. Rawlet, *Christian Monitor*, p. 53; Allestree, *Whole Duty*, p. 284; idem, *Gentleman's Calling*, p. 56; idem, *Causes of the Decay*, pp. 106, 349; Taylor, *Holy Living*, pp. 89, 203.
6. *Causes of the Decay*, pp. 213, 35; *Gentleman's Calling*, pp. 31–35, 124, 130.
7. Howell, *Common-Prayer-Book*, sigs. A2–A4v; William Sherlock, *Practical Discourse*, p. 182; Dawes, *Great Duty*, pp. 22–36; G. B., *Weeks Preparation*, sig. A7.
8. Only Vincent's book made Dissenters higher on I14.
9. Vincent, *Gods Terrible Voice*, pp. 14–15, 10–11.
10. Only Stanley gave Anglicans the advantage with I17.

distress. Later works were still troubled primarily by vice and by superstition or ignorance (I17), meaning popery.[11] Unbelief (I19) still did not seem as great a threat as superstition, unless increasing attention to the duty of belief (F3) is taken into account. Writing early in the century, Smith had supposed that under persecution the nation would relapse into popish superstition, as it had under Queen Mary. Faced with the same menace in 1688, Stanley scoffed that the Roman Church could not hold even its own leaders, who were drifting into Quietism in their disgust.[12] But, of course, there would have been no need for his book except for the fear that the English would abandon their Church to follow James II back into popery. Atheism might be the newer threat, but superstition still had the bigger battalions.

Hart's tracts, which probably reached the lowest stratum of the reading public, were largely given over to these various fears. It was deplorable, he thought, that the nation of God's greatest mercies should have become a very Sodom of treachery, fleshliness, and pride. Even the children were old in sin.[13] Many still went to church for fashion's sake, but it was an age of atheism. And in these last and worst days of the world, England could expect to be punished in proportion to her former blessings. Already he saw the fulfillment of the prophecies in Titus, Jude, and 2 Peter, when Quakers, Shakers, and Ranters turned liberty of conscience into liberty for their lusts.[14] The plagues of famine and sword raged in Ireland and Germany. And religious persecutions in Savoy indicated that Judgment had begun, though he hoped there might still be time for England to repent.[15] Other authors were more restrained, but would not have considered these fears outlandish.[16]

This fascination with vice or blasphemy is often taken as evidence of psychological vulnerability. Such an unconscious compensation may explain the tendency of some Dissenters to single out atheism as their most intense fear. The more their faith was intellectualized,

11. Only Stanley gave the later period its lead in reference to superstition, but even without him it was the highest among the concerns of the later works.
12. Smith, *Great Assize*, pp. 368–70; Stanley, *Faith and Practice*, pp. 118–19.
13. *Plain Mans Plain path-way*, sigs. A8, A3ᵛ; *Dooms-day*, sig. A5.
14. *Black Book*, pp. 6, 12; *Christ's First Sermon*, sig. C2.
15. *Plain Mans Plain path-way*, sigs. A3ᵛ, A8ᵛ, B3ᵛ.
16. Bayly, *Practice of Piety*, sig. A2ᵛ; Allestree, *Causes of the Decay*, passim; Vincent, *Gods Terrible Voice*, passim.

the more susceptible it was to doubt. Ball shrugged off the atheism of the early century as a fashionable pose, and others treated it in terms of purely intellectual doubts, as of the afterlife or hell, the existence of spirits, or providence.[17] But it obviously disturbed Brookes to hear men boast that they would rather perish with the multitude than go to heaven with the few.[18] And for Baxter the threat of atheism was deeply felt. He used the charge freely, as the most extreme and intimidating accusation in a writer's arsenal. By way of convincing the unbeliever, he cited the evidence of the fallen angels: "How came they to appear in terrible shapes to so many as they have done, and still upon designs that declare their own dejected base condition, and their enmity to God and man, and their eager desire to engage men in a way of sin? If any infidel will not believe that really there have been witches and apparitions, and consequently that there are devils, who are miserable, malicious spirits, who by sin are cast out of the favour of God, and would draw men into their miserable case; let them come and reason the case with me, and I shall quickly tell them of so many sure and undeniable instances, and give them so much proof of the truth of it, as shall leave them nothing to say against it, unless they will still say, We will not believe."[19] A belief that relied on these proofs cannot have been as secure as the "implicit faith" which the Dissenters derided, and this insecurity may have prompted a compulsive anxiety about others.

To combat the spread of irreligion, both parties looked to the family. Especially after the Revolution, the importance of family catechizing and devotions was recommended (H5), to make children proof against the scepticism and immorality that they would meet in society. Dissenters had long recognized this need. The earliest of their popular works had asserted the family's primacy as a political, educational, and religious unit. A well-ordered family ought to be a church in miniature, discussing the sermon and singing Psalms together. The survival of Dissent was no doubt due in large part to this alternative institutional basis. But, toward the end of the century, Russell worried that family devotions had fallen off

17. Ball, *Short Treatise*, p. 47; Smith, *Great Assize*, pp. 156–58; Brookes, *Apples of Gold*, p. 207; Baxter, *Call to the Unconverted*, pp. 527–28; also Anglicans Lake, *Officium*, p. 113; William Sherlock, *Practical Discourse*, p. 182.

18. *Apples of Gold*, pp. 326–28.

19. *Call to the Unconverted*, p. 506.

even among "the best of People." He warned that nothing else would bring peace, prosperity, or national "Reformation."[20]

Popular Anglican works gave even greater thought to the management of children. The Whole Duty of Man was more a family book than any of the Dissenting best sellers, which had tended more toward evangelical and individual concerns. Four of the Anglican best sellers were catechisms, while Ken and Patrick wrote for youths at the stage of separation from their parents. Of course, the moralistic Anglicans were concerned to preserve the presumed innocence of the young. But their interest began even earlier, with the prohibition of birth control and abortion, the enlisting of godparents, and the insistence on mothers' nursing their own children. They worried over a general neglect of discipline, where parents smile "to see the witty shifts of the child, and think it matters not what they do while they are little." Correction should be proportioned to the child's fault and his "tenderness." It must not be given in rage lest the child think it is for the parent's anger rather than for his own fault. But parental authority must be reestablished if there is to be a proper obedience to ministers or magistrates.[21] Even Anglicans were able to think of the family as "a kind of Church" and to recommend the catechizing of children at home by parents or masters as well as by ministers.[22]

Of course, Anglicans viewed the family as a preparation for Church life and not as a substitute for it. But they were now painfully conscious of the Church's dependence on popular support, and called on the leaders of society—parents and the upper classes —to demonstrate that support. Their money could help maintain a clergy learned enough to convince the gainsayers, and their prestige could help to keep up the hedge of discipline and liturgy. At the very least, they could keep their dogs out of the church during service.[23] Already Anglican clergymen looked back nostalgically to

20. Ball, Short Treatise, p. 191; Alleine, Alarm to Unconverted, pp. 166–69; Bayly, Practice of Piety, pp. 291, 407, 312; Calamy, Godly Mans Ark, p. 2; Russell, Seven Sermons, pp. 28–29, 193.

21. Howell, Common-Prayer-Book, p. 97; Richard Sherlock, Principles, p. 62; Taylor, Holy Living, pp. 63, 107–8, 127, 59, 159; Allestree, Whole Duty, pp. 177, 305, 310, 325–26; Patrick, Book for Beginners, pp. 617–30.

22. Allestree, Whole Duty, pp. 339–40; Rawlet, Christian Monitor, p. 43; Isham, Catechism, sig. A3v; Howell, Common-Prayer-Book, sigs. A4–A5; Lake, Officium, p. 17.

23. Stanley, Faith and Practice, pp. 65–68, 78; Allestree, Gentleman's Calling, passim; Richard Sherlock, Principles, p. 81.

the Puritan years when Englishmen had learned to treasure the
forbidden liturgy and make Anglicanism a conscious commitment.
By 1667, Allestree had to report that the private chapels that had
been thronged when an air of conspiracy hung about the service
were empty again, as were the churches.[24]

Each side blamed the other for bringing religion into discredit.
Vincent scorned the Anglican hirelings who had abandoned their
duties in London during the plague. Churchmen indirectly criticized the Puritan clergy by disparaging the fashion of sermon-going.
Allestree was doubtless thinking of a preacher when he complained
that "a *distorted countenance* is made the Mark of an *upright heart*,
and none is thought to speak the Language of *Canaan* that dresses
it not in an uncouth sound."[25] Mead admitted the Puritans' part in
the decline of religion by pointing out that when "Religion hath
been uppermost, therefore many have professed it; it hath been the
gaining Trade, and then most will be of that Trade." Many rats had
come on board when Puritans guided the ship, who were fleeing
now that they faced persecution.[26]

In the face of widening irreligion popular authors did appear to
restrain their attacks. Both parties encouraged respect for the clergy.
Indeed, Dissenters had even more to say on the subjects of the
ministry (I5) and spiritual counsel (I8) than did Anglicans. This
may have reflected the greater vulnerability of their position in society and even in their own congregations. Anglicans emphasized
devotion to the liturgy (I6) and the sacraments (I7), rather than
to the clergy, as the mark of Anglican adherence.

Churchmen hoped that greater attention to church manners
would set the right tone. They winced at "what absur'd things are
done in the time of Divine service," including the growing habit
of sitting throughout the service. The Weeks Preparation asked worshippers to remember that when they entered "the house of God,
which is the figure of Heaven we are to leave the earth and the
world behind us, and to have our conversation only in heaven"
(sigs. A7ᵛ–A9ᵛ). Their worship should be "with all *outward* reverence and low prostration of body" as well as "all *inward* devotion

24. *Causes of the Decay*, pp. 198–203.
25. Taylor, *Holy Living*, p. 164; Patrick, *Book for Beginners*, p. 629; Stanley,
Faith and Practice, pp. 72, 87, 95, 104–5, 192; Howell, *Common-Prayer-Book*,
p. 90; Beveridge, *Excellency*, p. 550; Allestree, *Causes of the Decay*, p. 145.
26. Mead, *The Almost Christian*, pp. 25–26; Howell, *Common-Prayer-Book*,
p. 90; Lake, *Officium*, p. 117; Taylor, *Golden Grove*, p. 599.

of soul."[27] Lake did most to elaborate this devotional method, describing prostrations before the altar and responses to the priest's words while administering the elements. Taylor would have approved of raising the temperature of devotion in this manner; there was no harm in sensuality so long as it was associated with worship.[28]

Some Anglicans had reservations in this regard. The Countess of Morton had criticized "affectation and singularity in public worship." Dawes's appreciation of the Lord's Supper was only for its "benefits" and stopped short of any notion of a participation in Christ's passion. Stanley was satisfied that the English service held to a mean between extemporaneous prayers and the delusion of transubstantiation, in which Christ was thought to appear "incognito." What better advertisement for a sober Church than to be crucified between these two thieves?[29]

Among Dissenters, only Doolittle wrote extensively on communion and even he concentrated on the mental preparation which was to precede it. But a typology used to distinguish a sacramental from an "ethical" religion failed to establish a significant difference between the parties. Nor was there a significant correlation of sacramentalism with the churchliness or moralism characteristic of popular Anglican works.[30] Once again, the largest difference was between the sacramentalism of the continuing best sellers and the ethical emphasis of the early period. There was also a significant variance between early and later periods, as social and ethical engagement declined. Sacramentalism had a very significant bond with an interest in God and with an approachable God, with passivity, confidence, and traditionalism, and with a lack of interest in society.[31] This set of attitudes perhaps best describes the devotionalism of the perennially popular works, those which were most secure in the public's esteem.

Puritans were famous for their devotion to the spoken word of

27. Richard Sherlock, *Principles*, p. 42. See also Beveridge, *Excellency*, p. 560; Isham, *Catechism*, p. 41.
28. Lake, *Officium*, pp. 63, 68–69; Taylor, *Holy Living*, pp. 159–60.
29. Douglas, *Daily Exercise*, sig. E11; Dawes, *Great Duty*, p. 10; Stanley, *Faith and Practice*, pp. 192, 104–5, 120–26, 179–82.
30. Sacramental/ethical religion (A2, C3, C5, D10, F1, F4–6, F8, G6, I3, I5–9, I13, I16, J1–2/A1, A5, A8, C2, C4, F2–3, F7, F9, G4, G9, H4, H13, I1, I10, I14, I17, I20, J5). There were also significant differences between Anglicans and the early period, and Dissenters and the perennial best sellers.
31. There was also a correlation with an emphasis on Christ.

God, which struck them as nearly sacramental. But the subject of sermons was less an issue with them than the sacraments. They gave it no more attention than did Anglicans (I10—1.2%), who sometimes belittled this aspect of the service in which the laity might register its opinion by seeking out congenial preachers. Actually, the difference between groups over preaching may be better registered in the fact that six or more of the Dissenters' works began as sermons, while only three of those by churchmen did.[32] By contrast, three of the Anglican works were written around the Prayer Book.[33]

The Sabbath itself was sacramental, being a foretaste of heaven's rest. It was an oasis of timelessness for those who were otherwise concerned with redeeming the time.[34] And the fact that the Sabbath excited the writers' fears of profanation shows their sense of the sacredness of this still point. But the more they held themselves to strict observance, the more they were aware of the indifference surrounding them. Bayly offered an array of numerological proofs that the Sabbatical laws were still in force, in that all important historical dates turned out to be multiples of seven. "Any man that looketh into the holy History, may easily perceive, that the whole course of the world is drawne, and guided by a *certaine chaine* of Gods providence, disposing all things in *number, measure,* and waight. All *times* are therefore measured by the *Sabbaoth*: so that time and the *Sabbaoth* can never be separated."[35] Oddly enough, popular Anglican works gave the theme slightly more space (G7). But the force of their attention was dissipated by other advice—to set aside Saturdays before communion, or to attend daily services, or to retire for longer periods of devotion.[36]

In the face of challenges to the Church and to religion itself, Anglican authors could not ignore the question of the state's compulsion in religious affairs (I4—3.7%). Some of their best sellers were forever compromised on this point by phrases penned under Puritan rule. Allestree had raised the possibility of civil disobedience when the magistrate ordered something "contrary to some command of God." He might have ignored this circumstance had he written

32. See those by Russell, Mead, Calamy, Doolittle, Pearse, Smith, and possibly Alleine, and by Anglicans William Sherlock, Beveridge, and perhaps Dawes.
33. See those by the Countess of Morton, Howell, and Lake.
34. Russell, *Seven Sermons*, pp. 150–61, associates these two themes.
35. *Practice of Piety*, p. 360.
36. Douglas, *Daily Exercise*, sig. D8; Beveridge, *Excellency*, p. 563; William Sherlock, *Practical Discourse*, pp. 152–61.

after the Restoration. Even so, he had allowed that the magistrate was "accountable to none but God."[37] The message was the familiar one of obedience or passivity, with a touch of defensiveness in the practical justifications of this delegation of God's authority. The crisis of the 1680s brought protestations of Anglican loyalty to James II but also the reflection that whenever God's church had lacked temporal aid He had vindicated it in a special way.[38]

Opposition to the principle of religious establishment was entirely absent. Even so acrid a nonconformist as Mead could acknowledge that "If Piety be without Policy, it wants Security."[39] Categories designed to record advocacy of the voluntary principle or religious societies were never used. The theme of toleration or latitude was mentioned only twice, by Anglicans fearful of attacks by Puritans or Catholics.[40] Only in the greater concern of Dissenters over persecution (G4—2.3%) was there evidence of animosity toward the state Church.

But despite a lack of argument, this was the area of the most decided divergence of emphasis between the parties. Typologies reflecting Troeltsch's church/sect distinction and Weber's traditional/prophetic one revealed the most significant differences.[41] The church-oriented typology was designed to show up a responsibility for society as against sectarian alienation. Traditionalism was associated with justifying religious institutionalization as opposed to a prophetic or charismatic immediacy. A third typology, social authoritarianism/liberalism, also showed a highly significant difference between the two parties.[42] Though the popular Anglican works were significantly more socially authoritarian, churchly, and tradi-

37. *Whole Duty,* pp. 290–91. See also Taylor, *Holy Living,* pp. 119–25, 141.
38. Stanley, *Faith and Practice,* pp. 137–38, 19; Howell, *Common-Prayer-Book,* pp. 5–6.
39. *The Almost Christian,* p. 109.
40. Allestree, *Causes of the Decay,* p. 286; Stanley, *Faith and Practice,* pp. 123–26, 234–41.
41. Church/sect (A2, E7–8, H2–3, H6–9, I3–4, I14–15, I18/A6, B9, D7–8, G4, H4, I1, I16–17, I19–20, J1). This typology also shows Dissenters significantly at variance with the later works, and Anglicans with the earlier ones, and both Dissenters and Anglicans significantly at variance with the perennial best sellers, which fell between them. Traditional/prophetic religion (A2, D3, E5–8, G3, G7, G8, H6–10, I3–9, I15, I18–20/A1, A3–6, A8, D2, D4–5, E3, G4, H4, I1, I10–13, I17). This typology also showed Dissenters significantly at variance with early best sellers, and Anglicans with perennially popular works.
42. Social authoritarianism/liberalism (E8, H5–8, H13, I3–6, I8–9, I14–15/ H4, H10, I1, I12–13).

tionalistic than those by Dissenters, these characterizations are relative. We shall see that the Quaker group was significantly more socially liberal than other Dissenters. Both Anglican and Dissenting works were farther to the traditionalist side on that typology than they were toward the churchly side on the other typology. For even Dissenters had been shocked by the enthusiasts' prophetic criticism of traditional institutions. And even Anglicans must have absorbed something of the sectarian rejection of the folk elements in the nation's religion.

Not only were social authoritarianism, traditionalism, and churchliness significantly related with each other and with an emphasis on society, but they all rejected religious authoritarianism, conversionism, and supernaturalism. The latter constituted a rival basis, the point of leverage from which the principalities and powers of this world could be moved. Traditionalism and a church-orientation also shared significant correlations with confidence and passivity, which was only to be expected.[43] The one surprise is that, of the three, only traditionalism was significantly correlated with sacramentalism.

Popular works took up social responsibilities in terms suitable to the small communities of pre-industrial England. Most of the writers gave some attention to neighborliness, usually putting their exhortations to charity (H2) in the negative terms of avoiding strife. Anglicans were much more insistent on this theme, as on admonitions to peaceableness (H9), generosity, and good works (H3). Dissenters surpassed them only in the advice to exhort or rebuke one's neighbor (H4).

Directions were rather general, and seem commonplace. Bayly tried to be as specific as possible: "If thou meetest one that asketh an Almes for *Iesus* sake, and knowest him not to be unworthy, deny him not: for it is better to give unto *ten Counterfeits*, than to suffer *Christ* to goe, in *one poore Saint unrelieved.*" Taylor's works were the most sophisticated in their social casuistry. In this case he held that it was better to give to a bad man whose life depended on it than to a good man who was not in such desperate straits.[44]

43. They also all neglected self. Church and social authority shared a significant correlation with intellectual authority. Social authority also had significant correlations with general authoritarianism and with a neglect of Christ.
44. Bayly, *Practice of Piety*, p. 438; Taylor, *Holy Living*, p. 190.

Nearly half the writers tried to give some guidance on business ethics (H13). But only in the casuistry of Taylor, Allestree, and Howell did it venture beyond elementary condemnations of sharp practice. Usury still came under attack, as when Allestree advised that charity might sometimes require a loan rather than a gift but that it should be without interest.[45] Ball, an old Puritan, thought it wrong to borrow upon interest for business, but surprisingly, he thought it was acceptable "in case of necessitie." His suggestion of legal recourse for wronged servants was not echoed in later works, when pains were being taken to put society back to rights.[46]

Social harmony implied a hierarchical ordering which could still be assumed without argument. Neither responsibility for those in one's care (H6) nor contentment in one's station (H8) nor even reverence for one's superiors (H7) were matters of real interest. Justifications of a static order were unnecessary, for everyone had seen the evils of ambition in the recent wars. Not only was ambition unseemly but it led to all other sins and finally to murder, perjury, and "great and public ruins." The Anglican moralists suggested that rank was part of the natural order, if not an institution of God's providence. Allestree's reminder that "God hath placed some in a higher condition than others" implied that He guaranteed the social order or was at least satisfied to govern through it.[47] Differences in honor among men seemed to be necessary "for the better ordering of the world," and these differences excused some extravagance in dress and in standard of living, "there being not only a *lawfulness*, but some kind of *civil necessity* for such Distinctions."[48]

Allestree's apologetic tone contrasted with Taylor's insensitivity toward the poor. Faced with the unequal distribution of the world's goods, Taylor alluded to the cares of the rich: "nothing but danger, trouble, and temptation." To the unanswerable argument of starvation, he reasoned that it might be the victim's own fault and that one could not expect a miracle if there were people to provide for any genuine need. But he hastened to break off the discussion with the reminder that "God hath not promised us coaches and horses,

---

45. Allestree, *Whole Duty*, pp. 381, 241; Howell, *Common-Prayer-Book*, p. 99; Hart, *Black Book*, pp. 7–10.

46. Ball, *Short Treatise*, pp. 207, 194–99; cf. Patrick, *Book for Beginners*, pp. 619–20.

47. Allestree, *Whole Duty*, pp. 163, 210; Stanley, *Faith and Practice*, pp. 142, 160; Taylor, *Holy Living*, p. 85; Rawlet, *Christian Monitor*, p. 38.

48. Allestree, *Whole Duty*, p. 281; *Causes of the Decay*, p. 237.

rich houses and jewels, Tyrian silks and Persian carpets." One can only wonder whether readers accepted his assurance that "Poverty therefore, is in some sense eligible, and to be preferred before riches; but in all senses it is very tolerable."[49] Rawlet's clumsiness in handling these themes has already been noticed. It was exactly his casual association of rank and religious status that encouraged the objection which he deplored, that piety was "only for the Rich, who have little else to do."[50]

Others were more willing to allude to the duties of superiors, forcing them to recognize their oppression of the poor by adultery, corporal punishment, legal theft, and treatment of them generally as "creatures of another species."[51] Lake set out very plainly the clergy's objection to the values of a leisured class, in which "Pride is a point of Gentry, and having a just esteem of my self; that gluttony and pampering my flesh is a warrantable enjoyment of the Creatures; that anger and revenge are both effects of a noble mind that must not tamely put up [with] affronts or disrespects; that laciviousness is but a trick of youth; that the immoderate and expensive Artifices of cloathing, washing, patching, and adorning, about which so much time is frequently spent, are but the innocent setting off that beauty and comely feature, which they say, was purposely bestowed by God to be set out to best advantage for admiration and delight."[52]

Still, no one was simply master or servant; all were "Common-servants to the one Great Master," as Allestree reminded his gentlemen readers.[53] Children, servants, women, social inferiors, and subjects, all were in subjection in some sense, and Taylor provided the prince himself with a prayer to express his duty to his Maker. He warned even the well-born not to flout the authority of their own superiors or sovereign. For "It was never heard that the earth opened and swallowed up any but rebels against their prince." Even an angel might not revile a devil that had once been of a higher order, according to Jude 9, so serious was the issue of reverence for God's order.[54]

49. Holy Living, pp. 101, 106.
50. Christian Monitor, p. 52; see also chapter 3 above.
51. Allestree, Whole Duty, pp. 230–46; Gentleman's Calling, p. 73; Howell, Common-Prayer-Book, pp. 93–94; Isham, Catechism, pp. 48–56; Stanley, Faith and Practice, p. 144, et passim.
52. Lake, Officium, pp. 141–42; echoing Parsons, Christian Directorie, p. 393.
53. Gentleman's Calling, p. 112.
54. Holy Living, pp. 141, 75, 120–21.

From the beginning, Englishmen were encouraged to think of themselves and others in a vertical pattern. Ken taught children to pray that God would "Make me grateful to my Benefactors, friendly to my equals, condescending to my inferiours, compassionate to the afflicted, charitable to the Poor according to my enemies [means?], a Lover of good men, and kind to my enemies." In such a society, it was necessary for the Countess of Morton to remind herself continually to "demean your self affably and peaceably towards all those with whom you shall have just occasion to converse." And it was apparently possible to thank God for one's social advantages and the leisure for daily devotions—"which many good people have not the opportunity of"—without twinges of guilt.[55]

There was scarcely any mention of social mobility, leveling, or contractual responsibilities (H10), which would imply an essential equality among men. Even Dissenters, who displayed almost no interest in the themes of social submissiveness, implied that only heaven would see an end to distinctions of rank.[56] What envy was apparent was of religious privilege and not of social rank.

Of course, Christians had a common bond of profession, which Baxter honored rather self-consciously in asserting that on the subject of conversion "papists and baptists, and every sect among us, that deserve to be called christians, are all agreed in this that I have said."[57] There was a world beyond for which there was little of such feeling. Several Anglicans remembered to provide prayers that "Jews, Turks, Infidels, and Hereticks" might be enlightened.[58] But after praying that God would "take from them all ignorance, hardness of heart, and contempt of thy word," they said almost nothing of the Church's duty to evangelize the world (I1). Allestree lamented that aside from the efforts of the Spanish, whose greed outran their devotion, "How many ages must we look back to find a Man that has made it his business to convert *Infidels* to the Faith?"[59]

55. Ken, *Manual of Prayers*, pp. 40–41; Douglas, *Daily Exercise*, sig. B12v; Lake, *Officium*, p. 139.

56. Smith, *Great Assize*, p. 69; Pearse, *Great Concern*, p. 8; Russell, *Seven Sermons*, pp. 188–93; Rawlet, *Christian Monitor*, p. 53.

57. *Call to the Unconverted*, p. 514.

58. Taylor, *Golden Grove*, p. 638; Allestree, *Whole Duty*, p. 467; Ken, *Manual of Prayers*, p. 58; Howell, *Common-Prayer-Book*, p. 15; Stanley, *Faith and Practice*, p. 127; Lake, *Officium*, p. 40.

59. Howell, *Common-Prayer-Book*, p. 15; Allestree, *Causes of the Decay*, pp. 306–7.

In fact, the foundations of English missionary enterprise were just then being laid. But there was no hint of this vision in the popular literature, unless we count the distribution of these cheap religious works as the first step in that effort. Indeed, the same men were active in both the efforts of the S.P.C.K. and the Society for the Propagation of the Gospel in Foreign Parts. It is a matter of some surprise that this activity could have begun in a period of such apparent unassertiveness in religious matters. The faith that prompted such expansiveness could not have been born from presumption.[60] For Englishmen had just been shaken out of the habit of confusing religious and national identities. It was becoming impossible for men to "call themselves *Christians* as they do *French* or *English*, only because they were born within such a territory."[61] Even Anglicans felt besieged, as was shown in Beveridge's call to churchmen to proselytize for the Prayer Book and show "our Readiness to defend them [the Creed and the Gospel], to the utmost of our Power against all Opposition whatsoever."[62]

The limit of the popular authors' missionary ambitions appeared in Stanley's repeated urging to "countenance religion" by attending communion.[63] There were no proposals for reuniting Christians or evangelizing the larger world, any more than there were plans for helping the needy. Some were saddened by seeing how few nations professed Christianity, and blamed the divisions within Christendom for this spectacle.[64] Stanley did not despair of the conversion even of Jews and Turks, thinking it had been delayed only by the repugnant Catholic devotion to graven images. But he and Calamy thoughtlessly made "Blackamore" a derisive expression for spiritual outcasts, and were indignant at the image of the Virgin Mary at Loretto, for she "certainly was no Blackamore."[65] Any feeling of common humanity was limited to holding up heathen righteousness as a reproach to English libertines. And the fact that God had enlightened Englishmen with the Gospel, "of which the greatest part

---

60. Ford K. Brown, *Fathers of the Victorians* (Cambridge, 1961), pp. 382–89, 529, treats the later missionary movement as a compensation for a fading conviction, a search for faith rather than a triumph of faith.
61. Allestree, *Causes of the Decay*, p. 42.
62. *Excellency*, pp. 560–62.
63. *Faith and Practice*, pp. 68, 75, 87, 99–100, 170.
64. Rawlet, *Christian Monitor*, p. 1; Allestree, *Causes of the Decay*, p. 307.
65. Stanley, *Faith and Practice*, p. 127; Calamy, *Godly Mans Ark*, sig. A8.

of the world is totally ignorant," seemed cause for satisfaction rather than concern.[66]

Only the books with an early popularity were much taken up with the categories showing a social interest.[67] In fact, they devoted more space to these matters than they did to a consideration of God, though far less than that given to self. As expected, Anglican works proved more interested in society than Dissenters did, but there were no significant differences in this regard.

The correlations of social interest with other typologies are quite striking, however. A social emphasis blotted out the more devotional themes, being significantly correlated with a neglect of God and the self, with a fear of God, and with a rejection of both conversionist and sacramental piety. In its own context, a social interest was related to social authoritarianism, and to a traditional and churchly allegiance. And it tended significantly toward an active, anxious, and relatively unsupernatural tone.[68] Thus it would seem that society and God were rival interests, if not equivalent ones as Durkheim suggested.

We have had little occasion to mention change over time in this area of social and ecclesiastical concerns. Injunctions toward social deference became more frequent, but so did allusions to social fluidity (H10). Religiously motivated attacks on the Church—sectarian or prophetic—lost favor over time, and interest in the sacraments, the most public act of worship, rose dramatically. But in general, the popular literature was less interested in the social dimension of religion as the century waned.

It was to be expected that the other groups should vary markedly from the best sellers in this area, since they, like the Anglican and Dissenting parties, were defined by their positions on religious institutionalization. All of them viewed society from a distance. Even Catholic works, several of them written by missionaries, never failed to mention persecution (G4). Oddly enough, they registered as sectarian in their emphases, though also traditionalistic. Their sacramentalism was not more pronounced than that of Anglicans, though perhaps it contained more conviction.

66. Taylor, Holy Living, p. 54; Allestree, Whole Duty, p. 255; Causes of the Decay, p. 26; Ken, Manual of Prayers, p. 55.
67. D8, E7–8, G4, H1–13, I1–6, I8–9, I12, I14–20.
68. There was also a significant correlation with religious liberalism.

Quakers were much the most interested in social themes and were the only socially liberal group, varying significantly from all others on this measure. They were the most concerned with persecution and the most interested in leveling ideas (H10). And they were the only ones to disparage the ministry, ritual, and sacrament, or to countenance spontaneity in worship (I13). While Anglican and Dissenting best sellers were more decidedly traditionalistic than "churchly," Quaker authors are better described as "prophetic" than as sectarian. Thus there was a second statistically significant distinction in Restoration religion, between the Quakers on the one hand and both Dissenters and Anglicans on the other.

Liberal authors proved to be socially authoritarian on our measure and did not provoke quarrels with state or society as they did with more vulnerable religious institutions. In fact, they justified their religious views as bulwarks against a more far-reaching scepticism which threatened even the social order. Their intention, apparently, was to detach the moral, as well as the intellectual, order from a religious basis which now seemed an embarrassment, and rest it more firmly in current opinion.[69] As a sign of this seriousness, they were significantly more "ethical"—as opposed to sacramental—even than the Quakers.

Social and ecclesiastical questions were not the ones that dominated the popular literature. Differences in this area had given rise to parties somewhat earlier. But the failure to resolve these differences, the strains of community life in an expanding society, the fears of spreading unbelief, or of renewed civil strife, encouraged men to turn inward by the late seventeenth century. The Dissenters' works seldom directed their readers' attention even as far afield as their own families. And if they did not attack the traditional ordering of society, they ignored it, deferring their hopes to the life to come. Popular Anglican authors avoided claims for the Church's polity or for the sacerdotal ideal. Instead, they encouraged respect for the liturgy, sacraments, and even private devotions. The Anglicans' success can be measured by the very paucity of Dissenting works among the later best sellers.

Yet the Church recovered a measure of confidence partly by limiting its aspirations. Some of the fears of earlier times were even then

69. See Roland N. Stromberg, *Religious Liberalism in Eighteenth-Century England* (London, 1954), p. 125.

being realized, in an era notorious for spiritual mediocrity. And, insofar as the Church scaled its expectations to meet the realities of English society, one can understand the decline in antagonism toward religious establishment. One might expect, rather, the disdain of those who were at last able to ignore the Church, and the gratitude of those who could finally express their allegiance freely.

8. The Popular Religious Mind

Until this point, we have been taking Restoration popular literature apart, to describe the individual books, to compare the groups of works which were expected to differ, and to look at various themes as they appeared in this literature. It has been possible to show differences, even at the most general level of interests and attitudes, which were sufficiently consistent to justify the statistical analysis. It remains only to ask what can be said of the literature as a whole, of the total impression that is left by this body of evidence. What were the dominant themes and the most successful typologies? And, finally, what can we say of the society which found its mind most perfectly expressed in these works?

In reassembling the literature, we observe a striking agreement as to the proper concerns of religion. In the popular works as a whole, 70 per cent of all codings represented only thirty categories. These bore on man's duty toward God, the health of the soul, the means of grace, and the afterlife.[1] Among them, only the authorized liturgy and the role of religious establishment occasioned any disagreement, and only the woes of the wicked and the admonition to neighborliness turned the reader's attention outward. The remaining space was devoted to questions of church and community, of history and the larger society, of God's nature and man's, and of religious knowledge and motivation.

Books popular through the whole period exaggerated this pattern by affording these same thirty categories an even greater degree of

1. In order of frequency: B1, G1, F2, I7, G5, D5, C1, D6, F4, F6, G2, H2, G6, E4, F1, J6, F3, J2, D7, G3, G8, J7, I4, I6, F6, F7, F9, D8, J1, J5. The sum of the frequencies for these categories was divided by 1.8, the average number of codings per paragraph.

attention (77%). Compared with others of the best sellers, these classics were even more notable for neglecting social or philosophical questions and for stressing devotional themes; their foremost interests were, in order, control of thoughts (G1), the person of God (B1), repentance (G5), reliance on God (F4), the sacraments (I7), obedience to God (F2), Christ as atonement (C1), the happiness of the godly (D6), the worship of God (F6), and control of the body (G2).

The works which fell in popularity had spread their attention more evenly, with only 65 per cent of all codings directed to the first thirty of their categories. In general, the earlier works showed a greater interest in society, while tending to neglect the soul's relation to God.[2] Later best sellers varied little from the general ranking except to emphasize the role of the established Church and to neglect categories expressive of a more affective piety.[3]

The Dissenters' popular works were as narrow in their interests as were those with a continuing popularity. Their favorite themes demonstrated their greater emotionality: conversion, the happiness of the godly, the control of thoughts, the person of God, the unhappiness of the ungodly, death, prayer, and hell.[4] Judgment (J5) and persecution (G4) were more in their thoughts, and worship (F6), reliance on God (F4), and concern for others (H2) were less so, than with Anglicans. For Anglicans, the Church, liturgy, and work were emphasized at the expense of the Dissenters' interest in conversion and the afterlife. Their greatest interests were the sacraments, obedience to God, concern for others, the person of God, repentance, control of thoughts, worship, and reliance on God.[5] Once again, Anglicans showed less of the terror and wonder of Dissenting piety and more of their own characteristic concern for mundane duties and social imperatives.

As it happened, only the theme of obedience to God (F2) was coded for every one of the popular works. Except for works of limited interest by Penn, Vincent, Bunyan, Beveridge, and Allestree

2. Their foremost themes were the person of God, obedience to God, conversion, the unhappiness of the ungodly, rewards in the afterlife, and the control of thoughts: B1, F2, D5, D7, E4, G1. Their most notable divergence from the general ranking was in an emphasis on G9, I20, D8, and I14.

3. Their primary interests were the sacraments, obedience to God, conversion, the control of thoughts, the Church's authority, rewards in the afterlife, repentance, and belief; I7, F2, D5, G1, I4, E4, G5, F3.

4. D5, D6, G1, B1, D7, J2, G6, J7.

5. I7, F2, H2, B1, G5, G1, F6, F4.

(his *Gentleman's Calling*), all of the books also mentioned God's love, Christ's atonement, repentance, watchfulness over thoughts and actions, improvement in virtue, and the whole range of man's duties toward God.[6] This list could serve as an outline of many of the works.

The twenty-six least-used categories taken together would only have been equivalent to the normal attention given to the atonement or conversion or the happiness of the godly (5 per cent of paragraphs). Of these neglected themes, the greatest number represented such liberal attitudes as toleration, spontaneity, originality, or simplicity in religion, or social leveling, business ethics, and the well-being of society as a motive. There was very little interest in historical categories such as creation itself, the covenants, God's kingdom, historical evidences or causation, the festivals of the Church, or its mission to the world. The doctrine of the incarnation, intimations of the Spirit, witchcraft, and angels may have seemed too esoteric for the popular mind.

Apparently, it was not the variety of subjects that interested the general reader but the variety of treatment of a small circle of ideas and imperatives concerning the doctrine of grace—God's favor to His people—and man's response to it. Anything else was valued in relation to its bearing on this subject. A reader with a disinterested curiosity about theology, ethics, history, or social questions would have turned to other works. But until the end of our period the market for these manuals of devotion and spiritual direction was greater even than that for a literature of entertainment.

Assessing the Typologies

Those who search for factors or typologies which might prove to be the basic traits of human response are frequently warned against rigid classification. Indeed this rigidity has been criticized for showing "traditional" thinking. No better evidence could be given of the urge to categorize than this discovery of a typifying type![7] The defining characteristic of Rokeach's "closed-minded" individuals and

6. B1, C1, G5, G1–3, F1–7, F9.
7. Edward Tiryakian, "Typologies," in *International Encyclopedia of the Social Sciences*, ed. David Sills, 17 vols. (New York, 1968), 16:182; Milton Rokeach, et al., *The Open and Closed Mind* (New York, 1960), pp. 10, 40–50, 410; Howard Becker, *Through Values to Social Interpretation* (Durham, N.C., 1950), pp. 252–53.

Becker's "sacred" or "traditional" groups is just such a conceptual rigidity. It was because of this danger that the present study has dealt with all the more prominent typologies proposed, to see which made the best sense of seventeenth-century attitudes.

In assessing their relative success, we may first ask whether there was a general authoritarianism expressing this very mental rigidity within Restoration culture. Although intellectual, social, and religious authoritarianism were in conflict, when they were combined all of the best sellers were seen to be heavily authoritarian except Allestree's sometimes fawning *The Gentleman's Calling.* Later works were least so, but only those by Quakers differed significantly from others or appeared "liberal" on balance.[8] This general authoritarianism was significantly related only with anxiety and a neglect of God. Beyond these correlations, only an emphasis on society approached a significant relation. In short, authoritarianism seemed to be a function of social apprehension more than of religious devotion.

The least useful of the typologies in discriminating between periods or religious parties were those dealing with the major distributions of emphasis—to God, Christ, self, society, or the afterlife. They did not indicate any significant differences between groups of the popular literature. Other typologies indicating tendencies toward passivity, supernaturalism, and a generalized authority likewise failed to show up significant differences between these groupings. The more specifically doctrinal typologies of conversionism and religious authoritarianism, along with anxiety, divided Dissenters and Anglicans at the .05 level of significance. And other typologies indicated variances significant even at the .01 level: New-Testament emphasis, the perception of God, sacramentalism, social authority, traditionalism, and a churchly orientation.

In regard to the last three, the widest differences were between Churchmen and Dissenters, and this was the division which proved most significant on the largest number of issues.[9] In fact, only in regard to intellectual authority and the relative emphasis on God did differences between these groups seem negligible. Almost any page of these works would have indicated to an alert reader the

8. Liberals were significantly more authoritarian than Quakers, but significantly more liberal than Catholics or the perennially popular works.

9. The widest difference over church-orientation, traditionalism, social authority, conversionism, and religious authority was between Dissenters and Anglicans. There was also a significant difference over anxiety.

author's affiliation. The division between earlier and later popularity was comparatively unimportant in relation to our typologies. Only over Scriptural references and intellectual authority were the largest differences over time, and the latter difference was not statistically significant.[10]

Certain issues, between Anglicans and the Dissenter-dominated early period, and between Dissenters and the later period, apparently showed both a time and denominational difference, as Dissenting literature fell in popularity. The largest variance over anxiety, and significant differences over sacramentalism and the perception of God, fall into this category. We have seen that these typologies—confidence, sacramentalism, and a benign image of God —were bound together with passivity and an emphasis on God to form a devotional and dependent piety. With all of these typologies but the first, the largest difference fell between the earlier period and the long-term best sellers.[11] This seems to indicate a devotional middle ground which changed little over time and avoided the extremes of either party.[12] The existence of this middle ground or common orthodoxy qualifies somewhat our conclusion that the party difference proved the most obvious one in the literature. And whether the most glaring differences were the most important ones is still another matter.

Another way of assessing the salience of these typologies is to see which ones were most independent of others and which were re-

10. There were other significant differences over time in regard to anxiety, the perception of God, and sacramentalism.

11. The long-term best sellers also differed significantly from other periods over anxiety and scriptural references. And they varied significantly from both parties over conversionism and traditionalism, so wide was the party difference over these attitudes. There were other significant differences—with Dissenters over the perception of God, anxiety, and sacramentalism, and with Anglicans over religious authority and churchliness.

12. The typologies of this devotional or God-reliant mentality were correlated with a relative naturalism, and traditionalism. There were strong suggestions of a relation with a church orientation and a New-Testament orientation. Moralism/conversionism bore no relation to these typologies, and both Dissenters and the more Pelagian of the Anglicans (Allestree, Taylor, William Sherlock, and Stanley) were among the least God-reliant. The most devotional works were those by Thomas à Kempis, Themylthorpe, G. B., and the Countess of Morton, along with most of the others by Anglicans, and by Calamy, Doolittle, and Bayly among Dissenters. With all five typologies, it was the early period which proved least devotional. And, except in the matter of confidence, the books with an enduring popularity were the most God-reliant, and more so than Anglicans as a group.

lated to others in such a way as to seem determinative.[13] The most isolated typologies were a generalized authoritarianism, intellectual authoritarianism, and a New-Testament emphasis. These proved almost useless as indicators of anything beyond themselves. We have just been reminded that the last two were those which changed most notably over time. Apparently, a growing awareness of philosophical difficulty was independent of more deep-seated changes. An emphasis on God and the typology describing differences in God's image were relatively independent of other typologies. This would throw doubt on Œdipal interpretations of the religious consciousness. And indeed the more fearsome image of God did not have the expected correlations with conversion or with any sort of authority. The different authoritarianisms were negatively related to an emphasis on God.

Of all our typologies, conversionism/moralism and sacramental/ethical piety made the most obvious nominal distinctions between types of religiousness. But these typologies were only moderately successful in relating to the others. The former seemed to distinguish authors by party; the latter set the early period off from other groups. Some of the correlations which were expected failed to register. Conversionism was not significantly related to anxiety or passivity, nor was sacramentalism related to a church orientation or with the moralism characteristic of Anglicans. Religious authority and an emphasis on self also had only a moderate tendency toward other correlations.

Among those typologies which had a wider range of significant correlations were some which represented such basic traits as passivity, supernaturalism, and anxiety. Obviously, psychological factors were significant determinants in religious response. The other typologies with wide connections represented basic social attitudes: social authority, traditionalism, and a churchly ecclesiology. They seem to have been a reflection of an even more prominent factor, that of interest in society.

Of all the typologies, a simple concentration on society had the greatest number of significant correlations. It was therefore the best indicator of other attitudes. In fact, it failed to show a significant relation with only the three most independent of our typologies. We have seen that social concerns did not play a large role in most

13. See the appendix to my article, "Religious Typologies and Popular Religion in Restoration England."

of the books. But there was a distinct tendency for an author's social response to govern his other attitudes. Anxiety and conversionism, for instance, seem to have had social rather than personal roots, so far as we can distinguish these. All this might be taken as better evidence for Durkheim's analysis of the importance of society than for Freud's view of the importance of the father, in the religious consciousness of that time.

Interest in society was, in effect, the main rival to an interest in God. The typologies which we have just seen bound up with a concentration on God were as marked in their neglect of society. There was room within popular religious literature for both a devotionalism which ignored the world's distractions, and for a social preoccupation which reflected a more troubled, energetic, and authoritarian mentality. Each of these emphases, in its different way, fed the kind of pietism which characterized the evangelical revivals of the eighteenth century.

Conclusion: Personal Religion and Secular Society

Religion was the primary interest of the Restoration reading public, as it had been in the England of the Puritans. This much is clear from the unexpectedly large production of devotional, instructional, and theological works—to say nothing of Bibles, service books, and catechisms—when compared with any other forms of printed matter. After the Revolution, there does appear to have been a decline in the sales of religious works as well as a decrease in the length of those which became popular. But there is some evidence of a "moral revolution" in the last years of the century, in the effort of philanthropic Anglicans to distribute free religious books.[14] Even this activity suggests that Anglicans had come to recognize their homeland as a mission field.

For there were several developments in English life and thought which, even then, were taken as signs of secularization. The official toleration of religious dissent marked the end of any realistic hope that English culture could be given unity or guidance by religious considerations. Established sects provided a constant reminder of alternative standards of belief and devotion, forcing every thinking

14. Cf. Dudley Bahlman, *The Moral Revolution of 1688* (New Haven, Conn., 1957).

man to reevaluate his own religious commitment, or encouraging those who preferred to muse on the relativity of religious belief. As religion became a matter of choice, it found itself limited to private life and even to the individual's interior existence. Faith tended to shrivel from a matter of action to one of practice or habit, or even simply of thought.

This spiritualization of religion appears in popular literature as a shrinking of the intellectual and motivational basis, and as a growing neglect of society and history. Alarm over the present state of society, even over unbelief, fell, and a more passive tone came to predominate. Books were less colorful and were narrower in their interests. The emotional level of the literature declined as Anglican works replaced those by Dissenters, who had looked to the religious affections as evidence of a new life.

At the same time, a more comfortable piety was emerging. Later works showed less anxiety, less fear of God or Satan. Apparently the religious reading public did not demand new answers to the problems of social order or doctrinal authority. Nor was it given a more instrumental inspiration for religious duty. The very lack of discrimination in all these areas may be taken as a sign of continued strength, since efforts toward definition are symptoms of intellectual discomfort. The differences over various views of sin or of God, or of the sources of spiritual assurance, seem to have been nearly unconscious; they were never debated.

Concern for society was declining in religious literature just as the realization of secularization grew. No doubt, this decline encouraged the processes of secularization. An interest in social themes came to be incompatible with a concentration on devotional ones. Dissenters had turned inward when their specifically religious authority, which had been successful in opposition, did not prove sufficient for rule. But Anglicans were also coming to distrust the freer society of the Restoration, and were adopting some of the characteristic outlook of Dissent.

Where Anglicans differed most importantly from the more old-fashioned Dissenters was over man's nature. For, while semi-Pelagianism did not increase within a specifically religious literature, the tradition of Taylor and Allestree flowed on in the more imaginative moralizing of essayists, novelists, and satirists. A piety which Anglicans had associated with work and physical purity made the moralistic novel possible. And the fact that women formed a large part of the audience for this new literature may reflect the earlier role of women in patronizing the moralistic divines.[15]

In the eighteenth century religiously motivated authors chose to write from outside the recognized devotional tradition, perhaps perceiving that it was no longer doctrines that were in question but providence, religion, and ethics itself. Their tactical breakthrough meant a more attractive means toward emotional and moral gratification for anyone who had once used popular religious literature to that end.

For that literature had been austere. It was not enlivened by any flavor of a folk culture, and the luxuriance of supernaturalism had withered. The books were not written to make the reader feel good about himself, to reduce anxieties, or to revive flagging spirits. Nor were they meant to suggest ways toward gaining power over circumstances or to promote social success or national prosperity. Their function was to give meaning to life, to tell men how to meet God and walk with Him. Little was done to attract those who wanted entertainment.

Such single-minded devotion would crumble before the utilitarianism and naturalism of succeeding centuries. There were only hints of this change, in William Sherlock's popular theodicy and the scattered justifications of traditional authority and worship which we met in chapter 3. In retrospect, these hints of change seem more portentous than the more "significant" divisions between Dissenter and Anglican. For the most dramatic differences between these parties belonged to the past. They would not be resolved, but would fade into insignificance before a new controversy over the very basis and validity of the religious view of life.

Even Anglicans, who had the best of the ecclesiastical compromise, were turning to face the new threat of indifference. There was a greater self-consciousness in their attachment to the liturgy, as it came to be the badge of active churchmanship. They had found a new interest in children as the heirs of the future and were even then launching the charity school movement. But the best indication that they sensed the new power of lay opinion was in the books they produced, written with every intention of achieving popularity.

15. Watt, *Rise of the Novel*, pp. 43–47, 151–54; for the female patronage of Hammond, Taylor, and Allestree, see Doris Mary Stenton, *The English Woman in History* (London, 1957), pp. 167, 185–86, 229–37.

Popularity had not always been the goal of Anglican authorship. So long as the Church had retained the support of the government and the governing classes, it cared little about the attractiveness of its doctrine. But in the seventeenth century the threats to the institutional survival of that tradition, by Puritan, Catholic, and Whig, had led to a flowering of Anglican theology and patristic scholarship. Similarly, the development of a characteristically Anglican piety came only after a long head start in the field of popular literature by more Protestant groups.[16]

During his years in the wilderness, Robert Sanderson had dreamed of a restored Church preaching a cycle of fifty-two official homilies year after year, until Englishmen understood that religion was a matter of practice and not of intellectual curiosity.[17] But, at the same time, Taylor, Allestree, and others sensed the possibility of enlisting that very curiosity in the service of churchmanship, perhaps encouraged by the obvious appeal of *Eikon Basilike*. The decline of publishing by their Dissenting rivals was partly, no doubt, a reflection of their success. And from the Restoration to the end of that troubled century the episcopal bench was never lacking men conspicuous for literary grace and the common touch, a tribute to the newly discovered power of public demand.

16. See Anne Whiteman, "The Restoration of the Church of England," in *From Uniformity to Unity, 1662–1962* (London, 1962), p. 39.

17. H. Hensley Henson, *Studies in English Religion in the Seventeenth Century* (London, 1903), p. 207, mentions Tillotson, Patrick, and Burnet as favoring the idea. Croft, *The Naked Truth*, p. 31, agreed, and also suggested a standard Bible commentary "with a command that no man . . . teach anything contrary to it." Taylor wrote *A Course of Sermons for All the Sundays of the Year* (1653). Bray's standard parish libraries may represent a similar impulse.

Appendix

Coding Categories and Average Frequencies for All Groupings of
the Best Sellers and for Catholic, Quaker, and Liberal Works

A1   Authority of Scripture
A2   Authority of tradition
A3   Authority of nature, reason
A5   Authority of historical evidences
A6   Authority of individual inspirations
A7   Simplicity of religious knowledge
A8   Certainty of religious knowledge
A9   Progress in religious knowledge
B1   The person of God
B3   The nature of God
B4   God's government
B7   Natural causes
B8   The divine pattern in history
B9   The Kingdom of God, on earth
B10 God's creation
B11 Angels, saints
B12 Satan, demons
B13 Witches, mediums
C1   Christ as sacrifice
C2   Christ as teacher
C3   Christ as the incarnation of God
C4   Christ as judge, king
C5   Christ as friend, lover
C6   The nature of Christ
D1   The nature of man
D2   Man's fallen character
D3   Prudence reinforces piety
D4   Election, calling
D5   Conversion
D6   Happiness of the godly, in this life
D7   Unhappiness, false happiness, of the ungodly, in this life
D8   Man's resistance to grace
D10 The Holy Spirit and its work
E3   Desire for righteousness as motive

	All Popular Works	Popular 1660–1711	Popular 1660–88	Popular 1689–1711	Anglican	Dissenting	Catholic	Quaker	Liberal
A1	.018	.013	.016	.029	.014	.019	.019	.050	.141
A2	.009	.005	.006	.018	.014	.003	.012	.005	.087
A3	.008	.004	.018	.005	.007	.007	.019	.017	.139
A5	.002	.001	.007	.001	.000	.004	.038	.000	.073
A6	.002	.003	.003	.001	.001	.005	.001	.065	.008
A7	.003	.002	.005	.004	.005	.000	.000	.005	.039
A8	.007	.003	.006	.014	.009	.002	.002	.005	.071
A9	.001	.000	.002	.002	.001	.000	.001	.004	.018
B1	.078	.088	.092	.048	.066	.087	.064	.050	.025
B3	.012	.012	.009	.017	.011	.014	.010	.039	.112
B4	.012	.008	.014	.017	.013	.011	.009	.013	.025
B7	.000	.000	.001	.001	.001	.000	.000	.000	.007
B8	.002	.003	.002	.001	.001	.005	.007	.014	.008
B9	.001	.000	.001	.004	.001	.000	.000	.011	.012
B10	.003	.003	.003	.004	.004	.003	.008	.007	.014
B11	.003	.004	.002	.001	.002	.003	.009	.000	.008
B12	.015	.013	.023	.010	.010	.017	.005	.024	.014
B13	.001	.001	.000	.001	.001	.000	.001	.000	.001
C1	.052	.069	.025	.047	.054	.046	.059	.033	.015
C2	.008	.012	.001	.005	.010	.002	.013	.017	.033
C3	.004	.002	.000	.014	.001	.000	.004	.021	.001
C4	.007	.008	.005	.008	.006	.012	.013	.022	.068
C5	.010	.015	.008	.004	.007	.015	.011	.000	.005
C6	.010	.006	.005	.024	.012	.006	.014	.033	.143
D1	.009	.004	.014	.014	.011	.009	.009	.002	.027
D2	.016	.013	.017	.022	.012	.017	.010	.052	.027
D3	.010	.003	.025	.010	.016	.005	.001	.002	.001
D4	.016	.010	.019	.024	.012	.021	.002	.039	.004
D5	.053	.040	.065	.065	.013	.099	.005	.138	.004
D6	.052	.068	.043	.031	.023	.092	.041	.009	.002
D7	.035	.031	.056	.025	.017	.067	.017	.012	.002
D8	.022	.010	.046	.021	.007	.039	.025	.027	.000
D10	.016	.017	.010	.021	.013	.013	.022	.082	.031
E3	.005	.005	.004	.004	.004	.007	.000	.005	.001

E4 Desire for rewards, or fear of punishment, in the afterlife as motive
E5 Desire for material advantage as motive
E6 Desire for mental well-being as motive
E7 Desire for well-being of society as motive
E8 Desire for reputation as motive
F1 Love of God as man's duty
F2 Obedience to God as man's duty
F3 Belief in God as man's duty
F4 Reliance on God as man's duty
F6 Worship, honor of God as man's duty
F7 Fear of God as man's duty
F8 Union with God as man's duty
F9 Avoidance of sin as man's duty to God
G1 Control of thoughts
G2 Control of actions
G3 Improvement in virtues
G4 Persecution
G5 Continuing repentance
G6 Prayer, personal religious exercises
G7 The Sabbath
G8 Sickness, poverty, resignation to Providence
G9 Work, thrift, vocation
H2 Love of others
H3 Generosity
H4 Reproving, exhorting others
H5 Family devotions
H6 Responsibility for those in one's care
H7 Reverence for human authority, social degree
H8 Contentment in one's social station
H9 Peaceableness
H10 Social mobility, leveling
H13 Business ethics
I1 The church's mission to the world
I2 The church's unity

	All Popular Works	Popular 1660–1711	Popular 1660–88	Popular 1689–1711	Anglican	Dissenting	Catholic	Quaker	Liberal
E4	.043	.030	.056	.054	.038	.050	.091	.016	.025
E5	.007	.005	.012	.005	.006	.009	.010	.001	.001
E6	.012	.009	.013	.016	.017	.004	.012	.002	.000
E7	.001	.001	.000	.004	.003	.000	.000	.003	.007
E8	.016	.015	.027	.007	.011	.023	.009	.035	.017
F1	.041	.056	.021	.032	.041	.037	.045	.004	.010
F2	.076	.071	.070	.089	.090	.051	.043	.049	.037
F3	.038	.029	.038	.053	.034	.036	.014	.064	.103
F4	.052	.078	.018	.036	.057	.021	.036	.009	.006
F6	.047	.060	.022	.047	.062	.024	.051	.057	.026
F7	.024	.029	.022	.015	.022	.021	.021	.015	.000
F8	.016	.022	.011	.010	.012	.018	.018	.017	.000
F9	.024	.021	.024	.030	.022	.023	.026	.022	.007
G1	.077	.095	.056	.063	.064	.088	.080	.052	.002
G2	.047	.059	.040	.036	.050	.040	.083	.054	.005
G3	.035	.034	.032	.042	.038	.028	.062	.054	.013
G4	.014	.016	.014	.009	.005	.023	.021	.033	.011
G5	.064	.083	.036	.054	.066	.041	.040	.009	.014
G6	.043	.055	.023	.038	.039	.056	.027	.002	.001
G7	.015	.020	.006	.015	.020	.012	.003	.000	.003
G8	.033	.045	.025	.020	.029	.037	.044	.015	.003
G9	.021	.013	.045	.014	.028	.006	.014	.014	.001
H2	.047	.049	.038	.051	.069	.015	.035	.022	.025
H3	.015	.013	.013	.020	.018	.007	.014	.018	.002
H4	.009	.010	.011	.006	.008	.013	.006	.019	.000
H5	.006	.005	.002	.010	.006	.007	.000	.000	.000
H6	.013	.009	.017	.017	.022	.004	.008	.002	.005
H7	.014	.015	.007	.018	.023	.002	.004	.025	.014
H8	.008	.011	.003	.005	.010	.002	.013	.003	.003
H9	.009	.005	.014	.011	.013	.001	.004	.011	.000
H10	.004	.002	.003	.008	.003	.003	.001	.018	.001
H13	.005	.004	.006	.005	.006	.003	.002	.001	.000
I1	.003	.001	.004	.006	.004	.001	.003	.026	.010
I2	.007	.004	.006	.012	.011	.002	.007	.014	.004

I3   Importance of the church in salvation
I4   The role of the state and established church
I5   The ministry
I6   Liturgy, ritual, decorum
I7   Sacraments
I8   Spiritual counseling
I9   The Christian year
I10 Sermons
I12 Tolerance
I13 Spontaneity in worship
I14 Judgments on the nation
I15 Faction, schism, in present society
I16 Low spiritual state in present society
I17 Spiritual ignorance, superstition, in present society
I18 Heterodoxy in present society
I19 Unbelief, indifference, in present society
I20 Vice in present society
J1   The vanity, misery of earthly life
J2   Death
J3   Resurrection, second coming of Christ
J4   Millennium
J5   Final judgment
J6   Heaven
J7   Hell
References to the **Pentateuch** (Genesis–Deuteronomy)
References to the **Histories** (Joshua–Esther)
References to the **Writings** (Job–Song of Solomon)
References to the **Prophets** (Isaiah–Malachi)
References to the **Gospels** (Matthew–John)
References to the **Pauline epistles** (Romans–Hebrews)
Other references to the **New Testament** (Acts, James–Revelation)
References to the **Fathers, Creeds, and church councils**

	All Popular Works	Popular 1660–1711	Popular 1660–88	Popular 1689–1711	Anglican	Dissenting	Catholic	Quaker	Liberal
I3	.009	.004	.007	.019	.014	.004	.011	.002	.000
I4	.026	.014	.016	.057	.037	.005	.001	.102	.044
I5	.016	.013	.017	.018	.014	.017	.011	.079	.081
I6	.025	.038	.002	.024	.043	.003	.032	.023	.028
I7	.071	.076	.028	.100	.093	.046	.049	.038	.039
I8	.003	.005	.002	.001	.003	.004	.007	.000	.000
I9	.003	.004	.001	.002	.005	.001	.013	.007	.000
I10	.011	.008	.013	.013	.012	.012	.001	.002	.030
I12	.000	.000	.001	.001	.001	.000	.000	.034	.040
I13	.001	.000	.000	.002	.000	.000	.000	.012	.000
I14	.014	.004	.045	.002	.008	.022	.001	.001	.001
I15	.009	.003	.024	.007	.016	.001	.006	.012	.013
I16	.004	.004	.008	.001	.005	.004	.007	.006	.000
I17	.015	.011	.013	.024	.015	.016	.002	.037	.070
I18	.008	.006	.018	.003	.012	.002	.006	.006	.007
I19	.009	.005	.020	.006	.007	.010	.007	.002	.029
I20	.014	.005	.038	.007	.011	.012	.003	.034	.001
J1	.022	.028	.017	.014	.014	.024	.069	.008	.000
J2	.036	.043	.030	.027	.018	.067	.029	.000	.001
J3	.014	.013	.010	.020	.006	.021	.009	.016	.007
J4	.001	.001	.001	.003	.001	.002	.000	.000	.001
J5	.022	.019	.035	.012	.008	.033	.019	.024	.006
J6	.039	.039	.033	.046	.028	.042	.072	.002	.007
J7	.028	.025	.043	.022	.010	.052	.066	.005	.006
Pent.	.056	.049	.103	.025	.039	.076	.055	.056	.061
Hist.	.037	.041	.052	.015	.036	.032	.030	.011	.045
Writ.	.187	.212	.189	.146	.195	.185	.208	.087	.030
Proph.	.088	.081	.145	.047	.047	.140	.124	.185	.043
Gosp.	.224	.227	.184	.257	.237	.193	.224	.214	.273
Paul.	.268	.251	.218	.343	.297	.239	.151	.286	.309
N.T.	.114	.108	.095	.139	.114	.113	.084	.159	.150
Fath.	.026	.031	.014	.028	.033	.021	.123	.001	.082

Index of Authors

Addison, Joseph, 5
Alleine, Joseph, 41, 89, 93, 100, 104
Allestree, Richard, 13, 38, 49–50, 55, 57, 59n, 62, 66–68, 70, 73–74, 76, 83, 90–92, 95–96, 99, 102, 104, 108–9, 111, 116–17, 118n, 120nn, 121, 123, 126–28, 134, 136, 137n, 140, 142
Austin, John, 14n, 33

B., G., 39, 79, 95, 121, 137n
Ball, John, 2, 44, 61–62, 64, 75, 100, 119, 126
Barclay, Robert, 14n
Baxter, Richard, 21, 27, 47, 58, 74, 76–77, 94, 99, 101, 104, 119
Bayly, Lewis, 34, 57–58, 67, 82, 92, 100, 110, 123, 125, 137n
Beveridge, William, 44, 55, 58, 68, 73, 85, 97, 129, 134
Biddle, John, 14n, 86
Bray, Thomas, 22, 24, 53n, 142n
Brookes, Thomas, 47, 57–58, 61, 67, 119
Bunyan, John, 42, 57, 77, 91, 100, 102, 104, 116, 134
Burrough, Edward, 14n

Calamy, Edmund, 40, 57–58, 66–67, 75, 77, 79, 82, 92–93, 101, 103, 107, 129, 137n
Calamy, Edmund III, 47
Calvin, John, 33, 48, 54, 67, 82, 92–94, 97–98, 103, 111, 113
Croft, Herbert, 14n, 70, 142n

Dawes, William, 56, 77, 108, 122
Doolittle, Thomas, 40, 76, 79, 90, 94, 99–101, 104, 107, 110, 122, 137n
Dorrington, Theophilus, 14n
Douglas, Anne, Countess of Morton, 39, 56, 94, 122, 128, 137n
Drexel, Jeremias, 14n

Fox, George, 14n
Foxe, John, 58, 58n, 68
Francis de Sales, 14n, 37

Hammond, Henry, 13, 31n, 99
Hart, John, 45–47, 57–58, 62, 73–74, 90, 94, 101, 118
Howell, William, 56, 63, 82, 127

Isham, Zacheus, 55, 57

Jones, Andrew, 45, 45n
Jones, William, 45, 45n

Ken, Thomas, 43, 57, 66, 80, 91–92, 95, 120, 128
King, Gregory, 21, 29–31

Lake, Edward, 43, 66, 80–81, 91, 96, 122
L'Estrange, Roger, 10
Locke, John, 6, 14n, 61, 70, 77

Mead, Matthew, 51, 58, 63, 67, 76–77, 99, 101, 104, 111, 121, 124
Morton, Countess of. See Douglas, Anne

UNIVERSITY OF FLORIDA MONOGRAPHS

Social Sciences

1. *The Whigs of Florida, 1845–1854,* by Herbert J. Doherty, Jr.
2. *Austrian Catholics and the Social Question, 1918–1933,* by Alfred Diamant
3. *The Siege of St. Augustine in 1702,* by Charles W. Arnade
4. *New Light on Early and Medieval Japanese Historiography,* by John A. Harrison
5. *The Swiss Press and Foreign Affairs in World War II,* by Frederick H. Hartmann
6. *The American Militia: Decade of Decision, 1789–1800,* by John K. Mahon
7. *The Foundation of Jacques Maritain's Political Philosophy,* by Hwa Yol Jung
8. *Latin American Population Studies,* by T. Lynn Smith
9. *Jacksonian Democracy on the Florida Frontier,* by Arthur W. Thompson
10. *Holman Versus Hughes: Extension of Australian Commonwealth Powers,* by Conrad Joyner
11. *Welfare Economics and Subsidy Programs,* by Milton Z. Kafoglis
12. *Tribune of the Slavophiles: Konstantin Aksokov,* by Edward Chmielewski
13. *City Managers in Politics: An Analysis of Manager Tenure and Termination,* by Gladys M. Kammerer, Charles D. Farris, John M. DeGrove, and Alfred B. Clubok
14. *Recent Southern Economic De-*velopment as Revealed by the Changing Structure of Employment, by Edgar S. Dunn, Jr.
15. *Sea Power and Chilean Independence,* by Donald E. Worcester
16. *The Sherman Antitrust Act and Foreign Trade,* by Andre Simmons
17. *The Origins of Hamilton's Fiscal Policies,* by Donald F. Swanson
18. *Criminal Asylum in Anglo-Saxon Law,* by Charles H. Riggs, Jr.
19. *Colonia Barón Hirsch, A Jewish Agricultural Colony in Argentina,* by Morton D. Winsberg
20. *Time Deposits in Present-Day Commercial Banking,* by Lawrence L. Crum
21. *The Eastern Greenland Case in Historical Perspective,* by Oscar Svarlien
22. *Jacksonian Democracy and the Historians,* by Alfred A. Cave
23. *The Rise of the American Chemistry Profession, 1850–1900,* by Edward H. Beardsley
24. *Aymara Communities and the Bolivian Agrarian Reform,* by William E. Carter
25. *Conservatives in the Progressive Era: The Taft Republicans of 1912,* by Norman M. Wilensky
26. *The Anglo-Norwegian Fisheries Case of 1951 and the Changing Law of the Territorial Sea,* by Teruo Kobayashi
27. *The Liquidity Structure of Firms and Monetary Economics,* by William J. Frazer, Jr.